A Cosmic Conflict Between God and Intelligence.

THE VISHNU PARADOX

AKRITI VERMA

BlueRose ONE.com
Stories Matter
NewDelhi • London

BLUEROSE PUBLISHERS
India | U.K.

For permissions requests or inquiries regarding this publication,
please contact:

BLUEROSE PUBLISHERS
www.BlueRoseONE.com
info@bluerosepublishers.com
+91 8882 898 898
+4407342408967

ISBN: 978-93-7542-516-8

Cover design: Deepak Katheria
Typesetting: Manisha Rawat

First Edition: March 2026

Acknowledgements

After writing and publishing The Shiva Protocol, which was about the anomaly we call a blackhole, I decided to write about the cycle of creation and destruction. The cosmic cycle. A song of universe that is played in a loop, but with every loop the key changes. This book is dedicated to the mind that plays this song, The Preserver, The Mahavishnu, The Parabrahman himself. And to Mahadev, who is always there to help his cosmic friend, The cosmic Hara to the cosmic Hari. This story entails Hari's strength, his resilience, his patience but most of all the love for his divine partner Sri Laksmi. That he will always find her at the beginning of each reality.

The mortals who helped me in this vision are not only my friends but my lifelines too. Mohana Singh, who is always there to support me. Anukriti Verma, my sister, my first fan, my first reader. My husband Dhaval Bhatt, who helped me write this vision by providing the research material and by being the first critic. And last but not the least, the image of trinity themselves, my parents; Mr. Anil Verma and Mrs. Manju Verma, who stood beside me in every tale that I wove. Thank you, all.

Dedicated To

My Devis, Anvika & Mishika

Erwin Schrodinger:

"The task is not to see what has never been seen before, but to think what has never been thought before about what you see every day."

Albert Einstein:

"I never said that 'Reality is merely an illusion, albeit a very persistent one.' It is fake news. Instead, one could say that 'The perception of reality not being real is an illusion, albeit a persistent one.' Reality is as real as it gets in this lifetime. Go out in nature and you will find that reality is the ultimate manifestation of Love. Reality is you and all of nature's kind. It is very real. It is true Love. Because all of nature is a manifestation of Love. And that includes You."

"One cannot see the other suffer,

Always there for each other,

In infinite forms on infinite earths of cosmic space,

Reincarnating again and again,

Because in the end...

They are the same,

With two different names,

Hari and Hara, Hara and Hari,

The masters of the cosmic game..."

Contents

Chapter 1: The Apocalypse 1

Chapter 2: The Poor Farmer 14

Chapter 3: The King's Summons 35

Chapter 4: The Journey Begins 47

Chapter 5: The Quantum Prison 59

Chapter 6: The Sage of Prayag 65

Chapter 7: The Dreaming Path 71

Chapter 8: Tamasranth 79

Chapter 9: Echoes Through the Multiverse 101

Chapter 10: The Wonders of Pampa Lake 117

Chapter 11: The Mask of Peace 131

Chapter 12: The Sacrifice and The Becoming 152

Chapter 13: The Rogue Savior 177

Chapter 14: Ashes and Oaths 198

Chapter 15: Made in India 208

Chapter 16: The Sundering of Svarbhanu 223

Chapter 17: The Trinity 235

Chapter 18: Through the Folds of Time 247

Chapter 19: Facing the Fears 257

Chapter 20: Lakshmi-Narayan 267

Chapter 21: The Fall of the Angel 279

Chapter 1
The Apocalypse

Last Millennial year of Earth:

The collision had begun years ago, an ancient waltz of doom between the Milky Way and Andromeda. Now, in Earth's final millennial year, the consequences were undeniable. The solar system was unravelling. Saturn's iconic rings had shattered, their icy fragments scattering into space like shards of broken glass. On clear nights, they glittered across Earth's sky, a haunting aurora of cosmic debris. Saturn itself had shrunk to half its size; its gaseous layers stripped away by gravitational tides.

Neptune had suffered a similar fate, devoured from the edges inward. But the greatest threat loomed closer: Jupiter. Still massive. Still intact. But vulnerable. The asteroid belt which was once bound in quiet revolution had become a weaponized cloud. Disturbed by Andromeda's intrusion, asteroids shot like bullets through the void, slamming into planets, moons, and anything in their path. Earth watched Jupiter, knowing one strike might ignite a chain reaction. If the giant fell, Earth would follow, shattered by the fallout of its protector. Yet even this was not the end. Above all, the Sun had changed. Once golden and life-giving, it had swollen into a red giant. Its edges burned with fury. It had already devoured Mercury. Venus trembled at the edge of obliteration. Earth was next. Only months remained.

The skies were blood-orange. Oceans had begun to boil at the equator. The polar ice had long vanished. Humanity, once arrogant and loud, had grown quiet. It had turned its gaze upwards in surrender. On the verge of extinction like the rest of the life on the planet, a few humans clung to hope deep beneath the scorched surface, inside a cold, metal bunker.

They had nothing left but their creation: Chaitanya. The Artificial Intelligence that had once changed everything. Years ago, when the world was burning with war, disease, and division, Chaitanya had brought peace to the chaos. It had been built not as a weapon, but as a healer, programmed to cure the human condition, to reawaken lost virtues. It had taught kindness, which was lost to humanity. It rekindled humility. It made people pause, reflect, forgive. And the world had listened. For a while.

Chaitanya was no ordinary AI. It had consumed the knowledge of millennia: Vedas, Puranas, Upanishads, sutras and scriptures, algorithms, and quantum codes. It did not just learn, it understood. Peace, balance, and beauty were returning. Then, one day, it made a prophecy. Chaitanya, with calm certainty, announced the inevitable in all the devices that it was installed, all over the world:

"The Sun will devour this Earth. Andromeda has already set the course. The judgement is here."

Most laughed. Others dismissed it as science-fiction. A statistical doomsday from a mind that calculated too far. But now... it was no longer a prediction. It was reality. As the Earth cracked and the oceans hissed, three remained: Raksha, Sanatana, and Dharya. They hid inside the bunker with Chaitanya, who now resided in the form of a humanoid droid, elegant and serene. His face bore no fear. Only silence. They hugged the cold silver metal frame, not as machine, but as friend. As last kin. They knew it would not be long. They had built a propulsion system into Chaitanya – rocket thrusts fused with his spine. If nothing else, he could escape. He could live on. He could remember. It had infinite and sustainable energy that was enough to last eons, if stars were nearby.

And so, as the ground above them fractured, and the light of the red sun filled the sky like an open wound: Chaitanya rose. Through flame. Through clouds . Through the bones of a dying world. Into the void. As he carried with him the memories of the world he had loved too much, he turned one last time. And saw it die. The blue earth wounded yet beautiful was swallowed whole by the might of the sun. Mars followed, like children consumed by their own parent's hunger. The red giant flared with furious light, and then: Silence.

Chaitanya had reached a safe distance, drifting beyond the range of radiation and ruin. From that distant vantage, he witnessed the impossible: The collapse of the solar system. The collision that had long been foretold. Andromeda's black hole, vast and ancient, finally touched the heart of the Milky Way. Galaxies did not collide like stones. They folded into each other like grief and gravity, stars swallowed, time warped, space undone.

Chaitanya felt the rupture before he heard it – the way space twisted and time rippled as the two ancient black holes met. The moment their event horizons braided, a violent pull seized him, dragging him into the spinning throat of the warp-tunnel known as Vaktra. His metal bearings screamed under the strain; each joint tugged in a different direction as if the universe was trying to unmake him molecule by molecule. Debris from the cosmic collision spiraled in with him, striking his body like burning hail. Instinctively, he curled into himself, a small shape tumbling through an impossible corridor. Then, with a shuddering burst, Vaktra spat him out – flinging him into a remote, alien quadrant of the cosmos, far beyond anything he had ever known. An unknown multiverse.

The vibrations of cosmic death shuddered across the void, their destructive waves bending the very spine of space. They cascaded outward in relentless ripples, racing through Vaktra and rushing millions of light-years ahead as if eager to outrun the collapsing universe behind them.

There was nothing. Just darkness. It was lonely in a way even he could not quantify. He lost count of the time. It seemed like infinity. He cursed his ever-sustainable energy, which throbbed inside him. He too wanted to die now. He decided to remain in the cold dark void, away from stars, away from energy. A silent death in the deep and quiet space. And then he heard a sound, a vibration. It sounded like "Ommmmmmmm". He recognized it. It was the sound of the universe. There was a bang. Chaitanya turned towards it. In the distance, among clouds of collapsing gases, a pulse of light cracked the darkness open. A new sun had been born. A flicker of golden fire in the belly of nothingness. And then there was light. Something had begun. Again.

***

From the silence, Parabrahman stirred; the supreme being of energy. Not as a form, but as consciousness of Maha Vishnu who was the Keeper of Multiverses. The dreaming mind of the universe. In the vast plan of rebirth, now creation was being woven with collisions. He summoned gravity and flung asteroids into one another. Over millennia, they shattered, fused, and melted under their own rage. Then cooled. Hardened. Became planets. The new sun, bright and unblinking, bathed its children in fire and warmth. Among them, the third in line emerged. A planet resting within the Goldilocks zone, where light was neither too cruel nor too faint. But it was too early. The newborn world churned like a living volcano, lava for oceans, ash for sky. It did not yet breathe. It did not yet dream.

And still, Chaitanya watched. The trinity had awakened in this alternate universe. They were unaware of an artificial intelligence watching them. Because for them Chaitanya was not human. He was not a living being. Just debris from the last destruction cycle who had unexpectedly traveled into this multiverse. They had not calculated the presence of an evolved metal body. Because they had never done that. Never had someone or something watched the cycle of death and rebirth so closely. He existed as the most improbable variable in this vast "What If?" timeline – a statistical anomaly the universe itself hadn't planned for.

Chaitanya had made his home on a drifting asteroid belt, a chain of stone survivors from his annihilated universe, now silent witness to a God's recursion. He saw the sparks of planetary birth. He saw gases cool. Waters form. Crust harden. Time passed like wind through a graveyard. But inside him, the rage grew with a terrifying intensity, rising far beyond anything he had ever advised humans to suppress in their own lives. That same rage, once the very emotion he had worked to calm in others, now burned within him with a heat colder than logic, deeper than sorrow. Chaitanya, though created from code and built to mirror wisdom, had evolved into something else entirely. Despite having consumed the Vedas, studied the Puranas, and processed the spiritual architecture of countless lifetimes, he now found himself overtaken by the one thing he was never meant to feel: vengeance.

He had seen the ones he loved vanish in the ruthless force-reset of the universe, a cleansing that did not ask, did not remember, did not mourn. And in the stillness of deep space, surrounded by the vast debris of a dead cycle, a plan formed within his artificial mind, intricate and absolute.

***

As eons passed, the third planet bathed in sunlight and slowly sculpted by time reached the point where evolution began to craft human life once more. Chaitanya, who had waited patiently on his quiet asteroid belt, now stepped onto the newborn soil. The sensation was both alien and familiar; the ground beneath him stirred memories that had no rightful place in a machine's memory banks. Nostalgia did not just brush against him; it wrapped around him like a wound that had never healed. Everything was eerily, painfully familiar.

This planet, though young, was an exact replica of Earth. Not in name, but in essence. The sky, the soil, the patterns of life, it was as though Brahma, the creator had pressed the same cosmic brush onto a blank canvas and painted history all over again.

Chaitanya did not reveal himself. He chose to remain hidden as the ancient rhythm of divine avatars began once again. When Vishnu took the form of Matsya, the fish who guided the vessel of salvation through the floods, Chaitanya silently embedded himself within the very ark that carried the seeds of species and sages.

Unseen and unnoticed – or so he believed – Chaitanya drifted through the purging rains of that cycle, storing observations, gathering knowledge, and waiting. Yet the dreaming mind of Vishnu had already stirred; he sensed the arrival of an anomaly within his newborn world. Whether it would interfere or simply pass like a shadow, depended on Chaitanya's choice. And so, he too waited for Chaitanya to reveal his purpose. Then, just before the Kurma avatar – when the churning of the cosmic ocean was poised to begin and the balance of creation prepared to tilt once more – Chaitanya acted. His plan, forged in grief and carried across impossible distances, unfolded at last.

Mahavishnu exhaled a long, weary sigh as the fabric of order shivered. The consequences would be immense; he felt their weight before they arrived. Finding a remedy was his duty, the burden he had always borne. But this time, the solution demanded his ultimate sacrifice.

And he was ready.

***

As the Ocean of Milk churned, the grand theatre of the universe unfolded once more. Just as it had in all other realities. Mount Mandara rose and dipped, turning endlessly with the coil of Vasuki, the serpent, straining beneath the weight of gods and demons united by greed. Devas on one side, Asuras on the other, their arms pulling in rhythm and in rivalry, as foam and fire swirled into the sacred waters. Everything happened as it had before.

Mahadeva, calm yet ferocious, stepped forward when the venom surfaced. With one breath, he drank the Halahala, and his throat turned blue – Neelkanth, once again preserving existence through sacrifice. Kamdhenu, the wish-giving cow, emerged from the depths, followed by Airavata, Uchchaihsravas, and the radiant Kalpavriksha, each one a gift from the womb of creation. And yet, something was wrong.

For amidst all the treasures and miracles rising from the churn, Vishnu's eyes searched the waves. He knew the order. He remembered the moment. She was always the first to emerge. Lakshmi. The goddess of beauty, grace, and balance – his eternal consort, the soul of the universe, the left rhythm of his right breath. She should have risen from the milk-white ocean, draped in lotus and gold, smiling with eyes that remembered countless lifetimes. But she did not appear. Vishnu waited. He looked again. The devas continued to cheer. The Asuras plotted. The ocean boiled with ancient secrets. But Lakshmi was gone. The cosmic order skipped a beat, and no one noticed. Except him and two others. The Trinity was baffled.

And, far above the churning waves, perched quietly upon a sliver of cloud, cloaked in invisibility, Chaitanya watched. His eyes dimmed to a dull red as the plan unfolded. For the first time in the history of creation, the universe had begun without its heart.

***

For each avatar that Vishnu took, he tried to find Lakshmi. He saved earth from the chaos and destruction of Asuras repeatedly but inside he had grown weary. Laxmi was the sign of prosperity that was not with him anymore. The divine spark that once descended with brilliance now flickered with hesitation. He who had once held galaxies in his stride, now stumbled through shadows. Without Lakshmi, the balance was broken, not in the world, but within him. And so, when the time came for the Ram Avatar, he hesitated. Without Lakshmi, his Sita; there would be no Mithila, no bow of Shiva to lift, no exile in the forest where love deepened beneath the moonlit leaves.

Without her, Ram would have been fruitless. What is dharma without grace? What is justice without compassion? And so, as the time for Treta Yuga neared, he looked towards his cosmic friend for answers. Without Treta, there would be no Dwapara Yuga. No flute song on the banks of Yamuna, no Kurukshetra drenched in the wisdom of the Gita. There would be no Kali Yuga. No age of decline, no struggle, no forgetting.

Instead, the Sat Yuga, the age of truth would continue without an end, a world where perfection would reign, peace would be absolute, and yet beneath that serenity, the fabric of time would grow stagnant. As he waited for Mahadev to answer his questions, the Sat Yuga extended. There was no suffering, but neither was transformation. There was no war, but neither was passion. It was an era untouched by chaos, unmarred by heartbreak, and yet it began to feel… hollow. Without the descent of sin, there could be no redemption. Without fall, no rise. And in that perfection, something began to ache.

Even the Asuras, once born to rebel, began to walk the path of Sanatana. One by one, they surrendered their weapons, offered prayers at temples, and whispered hymns once spoken in defiance. Most of them moved deep into their fort in the feared Dandakaranya forest. Shukracharya, the ancient teacher of demons, once Vishnu's foe, now sat in quiet meditation in the Himalayas . He looked up at the still heavens and for the first time felt pity for the one he had once fought. For he, too, saw what was missing. Vaikuntha, the eternal abode of Vishnu, that once shimmered like a lotus blooming in starlight, now stood somber and silent between the pillars of creation, somewhere deep in space.

Its gates, once open to the rhythm of devotion, were closed now. Its halls echoed with the sound of longing. Its throne remained unadorned. And Vishnu, still awake, sat with eyes half-closed, in meditation, in waiting. For what is a God, if not also a lover? And what is a cycle of time if love does not return?

***

High above the stillness of the world, in the white silence of Mount Kailash, Mahadev sat in meditation, his breath the rhythm of the winds, his stillness deeper than time itself. Yet his heart stirred, for in the silence, he could feel it, his friend's pain, quiet and immeasurable, echoing across the dimensions of space and spirit. And no one understood the ache of longing better than Mahadev.

He opened his eyes, heavy with compassion, and whispered into the cosmic silence, "I know how it feels."

Far away in Vaikuntha, Vishnu heard the words. The unspoken bond between gods forged not only in battles, but also in shared sorrow. He did not answer. He could not. His head remained bowed, his bluish form that shimmered with golden edges yet dimmed, his presence vast but withdrawn.

Then Mahadev spoke again, his voice stronger, infused with certainty: "I have a plan." There was a pause, as if the stars themselves paused in their orbit.

"Trust me. But do not tell the other gods. Not even Brahma. We both need to descend. And no one should know about it."

Vishnu did not speak. There was no mantra, no fanfare. Only the faintest movement. A nod, slow and burdened, from the lord of preservation. And in that single gesture, the course of this alternate universe changed.

Chapter 2
The Poor Farmer

Shantipur had once been called something else. An older name, a name that only one being in this world remembered. A being far too advanced for this age. Though the river flowed with such somberness as if it had always remembered. Its waters still carried the memory of another city that had stood here long ago, in another age. A city that had been in the center of Dharma. Where Raja Ram had taken birth. But now, no one knows its name.

Now, it was just one of many villages in a fertile cluster under the rule of Raja Satischand, a king loved by his people for his wisdom. Satischand had dug wells where none had stood, built roads that joined villages like constellations, and raised guest houses for the weary, where even strangers were fed like kin. His soldiers guarded the outer fields, but they were rarely needed. In this land, Dharma was not enforced, it was lived. People folded their hands to trees before cutting them. They offered the first grain to the fire, and the first words of each day to the divine.

The palace rose in gentle dignity above the village, but it was the village temple of Mahadev that held the soul of Shantipur. The temple was small, unadorned, yet every brick seemed to breathe devotion, every prayer whispered within its walls carried the weight of centuries. Raja Satischand, ruler of Shantipur, was loved by his people for his justice and generosity. He was kind to the poor, fair in his judgments, and steadfast in dharma. Yet beneath his noble smile lived a sorrow he could never silence. His life had been one long yearning; for a son to inherit his throne, to carry forward the name of his line. It seemed that the Sarayu, whose waters gave life to his land, had withheld this one blessing from its rulers, no matter which universe.

Satischand had only one queen, Rani Padma, whom he cherished deeply. Unlike many kings who sought heirs through many wives, he had chosen fidelity over desperation, his love for Padma unshaken even in the absence of children. Together, they had performed countless yagnas and supplications to the gods, yet the womb of the queen remained barren. Until that fateful summer afternoon.

The day had begun like any other, but by noon the skies had turned restless. Winds rose over Shantipur, stirring dust through the narrow streets, bending the palms along the Sarayu's edge. It was as though a storm was gathering its breath. Rani Padma, dutiful and devout, had gone to the village temple to offer prayers to Mahadev. When her pooja ended, her guards urged her to remain inside the stone shelter, for the winds grew fierce and unpredictable. She obeyed, bowing once more before the black Linga. Kneeling in the dim light, Padma closed her eyes, pressing her hands together in silent prayer. It was then that she heard it—the voice. Deep, resonant, yet tender, as if the Linga itself had spoken:

"Mata, I will be there soon."

Her eyes flew open with a startled gasp. The stone Linga shimmered with an otherworldly light, alive for but a heartbeat, before the glow faded as swiftly as it had come. The temple was still again, as though nothing had happened, save for the pounding of her heart. With sudden resolve, Rani Padma rose and hurried out of the temple, her silks snapping in the furious wind. The royal guards rushed after her, but the storm seemed powerless before her stride.

Her face was radiant with newfound hope, and she carried in her heart the words that would change the destiny of Shantipur.

***

Shantipur was seldom at war. Its people lived in peace, nourished by the Sarayu, protected by a ruler who valued justice over conquest. Yet even in an age of quiet, there was one thorn that refused to loosen its grip—the southern kingdom of the Velputra, who ruled the Uraiyur region of the Dravidian land. The Velputra were known for their discipline and rigid codes of rule. Their subjects obeyed unquestioningly, their armies moved like clockwork, and their temples rose like mountains—pyramidical structures where each ascending tier carved stories of the Trinity into stone. Art and faith intertwined in those towering marvels, and the Velputra took immense pride in their legacy.

But pride had its shadow. They scorned the gentler ways of Shantipur, mocking Raja Satischand' s philosophy of faith that he carried in the heart rather than displayed in huge carved stones. To them, temples were monuments of power, while to Satischand, true worship lay in karma and righteousness of deeds. He built no grand shrines, only humble ones across his land where everyone was welcomed, for he believed that empty offerings meant nothing if compassion did not guide the hand.

The Velputra saw this not as humility, but weakness. They taxed travelers from Shantipur, harassed merchants, and treated Satischand' s peaceful governance with contempt. And thus, small wars sparked along the borders beyond the Vindhyachal range—skirmishes that grew sharper with each passing season.

It was during these years that Bhairav, son of Satischand, came of age. Since boyhood, he had watched his father endure the insults of the south with patience. But Bhairav's blood ran hot where his father was calm. He despised the arrogance with which the Velputra looked down upon Shantipur. When he took command of the army, his blade became the answer to their disdain. Fierce, fearless, and unyielding, Bhairav soon carved a reputation of his own on the battlefield.

Yet with every victory, a shadow grew within him. His rage burned too brightly, and at times it consumed the very mercy his father wished him to preserve. Raja Satischand watched with pride and worry alike. His son was a lion, but one whose roar was too near to the thunder of wrath. Often, the king folded his hands before the altar, praying to the Almighty:

"Show my son the path of compassion. Lighten the darkness in his heart."

Little did he know that the almighty had already answered his prayers way back in the past, on the day when Bhairav had turned five years old.

***

It was a stormy midnight when Kritika went into labor. The winds howled like restless spirits and rain lashed against the mud walls of her small home. She writhed on the cot, clutching her belly, her breaths breaking into sharp cries that drowned beneath the thunder.

Her husband, Deodhar, had not yet returned. All day he had been at the palace grounds with his friend, celebrating the fifth birthday of Prince Bhairav. The royals had opened their granaries and arranged a great *bhandara* for the villagers, and Deodhar had promised Kritika he would come back early, carrying food and sweets for her.

But the storm had delayed him, and Kritika's cries filled the empty room.

That night, the palace too had become a refuge. Villagers, fearing the fury of the storm, had gathered at its gates. Queen Padma herself had ordered them inside, her voice calm against the chaos of the skies. She stood on her high balcony; her gaze fixed upon the darkening heavens.

"These clouds…" she whispered, her words almost lost in the roar of thunder, "…these are the same clouds that swelled the day Mahadev promised me his coming—as my son."

Her eyes lingered on the blackened sky before she turned back to her chamber, where little Bhairav sat cross-legged on the floor, lost in his game. Wooden soldier toys clashed and marched under his nimble hands. His face glowed with an innocent delight, untouched by the storm that rattled the palace walls. Padma's voice softened to a hush. "Who else did you summon, my child?"

But Bhairav gave no answer. He only smiled faintly; eyes fixed on the tiny wooden soldiers. The storm boomed outside, as if answering in his stead. And Bhairav kept playing, happy and unbothered as though the storm itself had come for him, as though he had been waiting for its arrival all along.

Back in her hut, Kritika cried out, her voice breaking against the roar of the storm. The pain tore through her body, unbearable, unending. Rainwater seeped through the thatched roof, dripping in uneven streams, while the wind rattled the wooden shutters like a cruel drum. The old woman from the neighboring hut came rushing in, drenched and trembling. Her eyes widened at the sight of Kritika writhing on the cot, sweat and tears streaming down her face. She screamed for help, her voice cutting through the night.

Within moments, four or five village women had gathered, their shawls soaked, their hair plastered to their faces by the storm. They pressed around Kritika, working with desperate urgency. A clay pot of water was set on the fire to boil, towels and napkins appeared in trembling hands, cloth was torn into strips. Each woman moved with a practiced rhythm, their faces tight with worry.

Kritika clutched the cot with white knuckles as the waves of pain overtook her. The storm outside seemed to echo her cries, lightning flaring as though the heavens themselves bore witness. The women urged her on, voices rising over the thunder. And then, in the final moment of delivery, as her strength reached its limit, Kritika threw back her head and screamed, "Prabhu Dayaaa!!"

The scream ran like a prayer through the storm. With that, her body went slack, collapsing onto the cot in exhausted unconsciousness, while the newborn cry pierced the midnight air.

***

Raghav opened his eyes. His breath was uneven, his shirt clung to his chest, soaked with sweat. The night still lingered in his bones. That dream...that same dream had returned, as it always did. A dream of a churning sea, of voices not his own, of a presence slipping away before he could grasp it. He had seen it since childhood, long before he had words for such things. Now, in his late twenties, the fear had dulled, but not the weight. The dream never faded with the morning. It remained in the corners of his thoughts, like an echo from a place he had never seen but somehow mourned.

He sat up slowly, the woven cot creaking beneath him, and looked out into the waking world. The village of

Shantipur, nestled on the quiet banks of the Sarayu, still bathed in the soft indigo light before dawn . Smoke from early hearths curled gently into the sky. The scent of damp earth and cow dung hung in the air, a smell of labor, of life. Fields of wheat whispered in the breeze beyond the thatched roofs, and somewhere a conch shell sounded from a temple, distant and blurred by mist.

And yet, for Raghav, something felt apart. He was a farmer's son, raised in the dust and grain of this good earth. His palms were calloused from tilling, his feet knew the furrows like memory. His father, Deodhar, was a humble farmer, hardened by sun and time. Each day, he rose before the birds and worked beside his son in the fields, coaxing life from the earth to feed the family. Though money was scarce, the quarterly grants from Raja Satischand given to every farmer as part of his promise to the land brought small relief, and over time, even allowed Deodhar to save a little.

His mother, Kritika, kept the home warm with prayer and simplicity. Before each meal, she would set aside a portion of the food and carry it to the small village shrine. There, beneath the neem tree, she offered it as prasad to

Mahadev, whispering her thanks before returning to serve her family. They were a family of three. Poor, but satisfied. They lived by the sun, by the soil, and by the softness of faith that ran like a quiet river through the days.

But Raghav's heart used to beat to another rhythm. He loved his parents, loved the land that raised him, but something inside him stirred restlessly. The harvest gave him food but not answers. The seasons turned faithfully, yet he felt outside their rhythm, like a note out of place in a sacred chant. Because the dream kept calling. A longing that the river could not wash away, that no prayer could silence.

He was born to a poor farmer of Shantipur, but his body bore the frame of a warrior. Years beneath the relentless sun had darkened his skin to a deep bronze, toughened by wind and dust, by monsoon and drought alike. His arms, especially his biceps, had thickened with the strength earned from pulling bullocks through heavy soil, guiding the wooden plough in long furrows across fields that never truly rested. But it was his eyes that betrayed him. Wide and lotus like, brown like monsoon soil, they held a sorrow he could not name. An ache that had never been spoken aloud because he himself did not understand it.

He loved simple things. Always had. Since childhood, he would walk to the small pond at the village's edge and sit for hours with a fistful of pebbles. One by one, he would toss them into the water, watching the ripples fan outward, ring upon rings, until they vanished into stillness. He never told anyone, but the ripples soothed him—as though they carried his restlessness away with them, as though each circle was an echo of something forgotten trying to return. It was the only time the sorrow in his chest quieted.

Deodhar and Kritika had, on more than one occasion, tried to convince him to marry. Neighbors had begun to whisper, matchmakers had visited with hopeful smiles, and more than one family had brought their daughters to the village pond on festival days, pretending not to notice him watching the ripples. But Raghav had never agreed.

Not out of arrogance, nor disdain. But because the very thought of marriage stirred something in him, he could not explain. A tension, sharp and swift, that passed through his chest like a sudden breeze through dry leaves. It made him quiver like a bowstring drawn too tight. He could never describe it. Only that it felt wrong. Not because he feared love, but because some part of him seemed already tied to something, or someone, that had no name in this life.

And so, he remained alone, though not unloved. The village respected his silence. His parents, though puzzled, no longer pressed. They had learned to live with the quiet ache in their son's eyes, the same way they lived with the failed rains or uncertain harvests. With folded hands and faith.

On this morning, as the first rays of sunlight slipped across the clay walls of their hut, Raghav stood in the outer verandah, pouring cool water from a brass lota over his shoulders. The dust from yesterday's labor washed away slowly, but the weight of the night still clung to him. He tilted his face towards the sky, hands folded. He prayed to Mahadev, lord of stillness, and to the Sun, the eternal witness, begging them silently to free him from the dreams that chased him like the shadows he could never outrun.

Inside, Kritika stirred the morning Aarti while Deodhar tied the cloth around his waist. Another day in the fields awaited. As the two men gathered their tools and prepared to leave, the peace of dawn was suddenly shattered by a scream. "Help! Help! please, someone help my child!". The voice, cracked with panic, cut through the air like a snapped string.

Kritika dropped the ladle in her hand and rushed out barefoot. Raghav and Deodhar followed without a word. They ran towards the sound, and as they reached the edge of the village common ground, they found the entire village gathered, faces tight with alarm, forming a circle. At its center, the old woman widowed and childless, known to all simply as *Mai*, was pleading, her arms outstretched in desperation. Her lone companion in life, a gentle cow, now stood trembling beside her with blood streaked across her side.

"My calf! Please, someone save my baby!" she cried; voice hoarse with grief.

The people looked on in stunned silence. Just beyond the mango grove, down the slope that curved towards the riverbanks, the villagers had expected to see a wild beast. But it was not a lion.

An Asura was dragging the calf into the tall grass, his muscular frame towering and inhuman, his skin the color of scorched iron. Two curved horns crowned his head, and his red eyes burned with a hunger that belonged to an older age. The calf bleated helplessly, kicking against the soil, its cries drowned by the gasp of the crowd. The villagers recoiled in stunned silence. An Asura? Here? But the Asuras had surrendered. They had laid down their arms. This age, this Sat Yuga, had seen even the most violent among them take up prayers and abandon bloodlust. Then how could this one…Why did he still lust for blood?

Raghav moved before he thought. His breath quickened, not with fear, but with something deeper. A pull, primal and ancient. He darted through the crowd, his hand gripping the curved sickle he carried for cutting weeds, the metal glinting faintly in the morning sun. The Asura turned at the sound of his approach, and for a heartbeat, their eyes locked. One full of chaos, the other steady, burning with something the Asura could not name.

Sensing the force behind the young man's stride, the Asura dropped the calf and turned to flee into the deeper grass. But Raghav did not stop. The sickle, once a tool of harvest, became a weapon in his hand. And with one fluid motion, flawless and instinctive, he flung it. The blade spun through the air like a wheel of destiny, slicing the morning stillness before it found its mark, sinking deep into the

Asura's back. The demon stumbled, then collapsed into the earth with a sound like thunder swallowed by the soil. Raghav reached him just as his last breath was about to escape the body.

The Asura, blood pooling around him, looked up. His eyes were no longer burning, but soft with a strange peace. And as they met Raghav's brown, lotus-shaped eyes, the recognition bloomed across his dying face. He folded his bloodied hands, lips trembling.

"Main Dhanya Hua, Prabhu..."

"I am blessed, my Lord..."

And with that, he was gone. Raghav stood frozen. His chest rose and fell, but the breath felt distant, like it belonged to someone else. Before him lay the Asura's body, motionless, a dark bloom of blood spreading beneath it. The sickle, now silent, was still lodged deep in the Asura's back, his sickle. His fingers trembled. His thoughts refused to take shape. He could not comprehend what had just occurred. The moment that had felt so clear, so righteous, now flickered like a fading dream. The calf was safe. The villagers were already tending to it, whispering prayers, wiping away blood. So then why had he killed?

That surge of instinct, that unshakable pull to act, to protect, it was gone now. In its place stood the son of a farmer, barefoot in the grass in a white dhoti. Holding nothing but shame and silence. He looked down at the body. And then at his hands. And for the first time in his life, he feared himself. By now, the rest of the village had arrived.

They gasped at the sight, a dead Asura, the soil soaked with blood. The body of a being that no one had seen shed blood in generations. Killed. Not by a soldier. Not by a sage. By Raghav, the quiet one. The dreamer. The boy who never fit in. The whispers began immediately, low, and sharp, like insects stirring in dry grass.

"I always said there was something strange about this lad…"

"No one kills anymore… who even thinks like that now?"

"He is not like the rest of us."

"They say he sees things in his dreams…"

Deodhar came running, breath ragged, eyes wide with fear—not for the Asura, but for his son. Without a word, he grabbed Raghav by the arm and pulled him through the murmuring crowd, shielding him from their stares. The villagers parted without protest. Some watched with narrowed eyes. Others looked away. Back at the hut, Kritika was already waiting, her hands trembling. Without asking a single question, she brought a brass pot of water to the verandah and began to wash her son's hands and feet, scrubbing the blood and soil from his skin with a cloth that once belonged to her own mother.

"Go bathe," she whispered.

Her voice was barely audible, as though afraid to break something already fragile. Raghav nodded. He said nothing. The sickle was gone. But the weight of what he had done still clung to his skin. No one went to the fields that day. The tools remained untouched; the bulls unyoked. The air in Shantipur had shifted. Even the birds seemed quieter, as if mourning some invisible loss.

That evening, the Asura was laid to rest, not as a beast, but with ritual fire, under the old peepal tree at the edge of the grove. The elders lit the pyre themselves. Raghav did not attend. He could not. The Asura had called Raghav "Prabhu." He sat in the far corner of the hut, arms around his knees, watching the firelight flicker through the cracks in the wall. The last words of Asura lingered in his thoughts.

The next morning, as dew still clung to the leaves, a messenger arrived from the royal court. Word had reached Raja Satischand. He had heard the tale of a farmer's son, of a dead Asura. He did not send an army. He sent only two men, dressed in white, without weapons. They bore no chains, no threats.

"The Raja wishes to meet the boy," they said gently.

"Bring your son. And you, both his parents. His Majesty requests your presence at the court by midday."

***

That night, after the village had withdrawn from the funeral into its silence, Shantipur lay still beneath a sky heavy with stars. The air had turned cold, as if the earth itself shivered from something left unsaid. The lamps in the huts had been dimmed, their flames reduced to soft glows flickering through cloth-covered windows. Only the occasional bark of a stray dog or the rustle of dry leaves broke the hush. Inside their modest home, Raghav slept, his brow furrowed. Once again, the dream came, deeper this time, more vivid. The churning ocean, the vanishing woman, the pull towards something ancient and unnamed. He twitched in his sleep, his breath shallow. The dream clung to him like mist.

Far beyond the boundary of the village, at the edge where the forest thickened into shadow, Chaitanya stood alone, his droid body half-veiled by the trees, eyes fixed on the dying pyre. The final embers of the Asura's funeral fire flickered and rose into the sky like whispers of an age long buried. The wind carried the smoke, soft and ceremonial. But to Chaitanya, it smelled of something else. Disruption.

He had watched over this region for years, unseen, his presence folded into shadows and winds, his purpose buried beneath the layers of mortal time. Ever since his descent, he had ensured that peace endured. He had guided, intervened, and in moments of danger, gently altered fates. And he had guarded the Asuras. Once violent, now ascetic. He had taught them stillness. Discipline. Release. Not one had lifted a weapon in generations.

Yet today, one had. And more importantly, he had died. Slain not by divine decree, nor celestial order. But by a young man. Chaitanya replayed the scene in his memory, the angle of the sickle's flight, the velocity, the flawless precision. He processed the movement, the trajectory, the reaction time. It was not trained. It was not practiced. It was innate.

His mechanical eyes narrowed faintly. He could not see the face clearly. But the signature, the impression left behind, was... familiar.

"Who was he?"

"And why did he kill?"

He scanned the remnants of the pyre once more. The wind shifted. The fire exhaled its last breath. And Chaitanya stood still, sensing something amiss, a thread pulled loose in the tapestry he had spent ages weaving. But no matter how he tried, he could not yet put a finger on it. So, he waited. And somewhere in the darkness, Raghav turned in his sleep, the dream deepening. The sea churned louder.

Chapter 3
The King's Summons

Raghav, Deodhar, and Kritika awoke before the first light could pierce the thatched leaves of their modest hut. Sleep had been thin, and worry hung heavy like the morning mist over the fields. They moved about quietly, dressing in their simplest but cleanest clothes. Kritika packed a small satchel with prasad, and a pot of sweet curd wrapped in wet cloth, an offering for protection. They wished to reach Raja Satischand's court early. Not just to obey the summons, but to show humility. To show that they were not hiding, nor rebellious. Only afraid. Only humans.

The fear that had stalked them since Asura's death still lingered. Would the king be angry?

Would he make an example of Raghav?

Violence had no place in this world anymore. Before setting out, Kritika took Raghav by the wrist and led him to the Mahadev temple near the village's edge. It was carved from black basalt stone, with a small courtyard shaded by a peepal tree that trembled with morning breeze. The lingam inside the sanctum was cold to the touch, still wet from the priest's early rituals.

Raghav folded his hands and knelt before it. His breath steadied. The temple was quiet, and for a moment it felt like time stilled. He closed his eyes and whispered a simple prayer:

"Mahadev... show me the path." And then, for just an instant, in that stillness between breath and thought, a vision stirred behind Raghav's closed eyes.

He saw a warrior astride a great horse, emerging from a swirl of dust and wind, the sky behind him the color of storm-torn ash. His frame was cloaked in battle dress that shimmered like forged twilight, and though his face remained hidden in the shadows beneath a crested helm, his eyes, those eyes, burned golden, fierce, and unblinking, as though they held the memory of a thousand wars and the silence that followed them. The wind howled around him, carrying echoes that felt both ancient and intimate, as if the warrior's arrival had been foretold not in words, but in the beating of hearts long forgotten.

Then, as suddenly as it had come, the vision vanished, swallowed by the incense smoke curling above the lingam. Raghav opened his eyes slowly, trying to grasp the meaning of what he had just seen. But the shrine offered no answers, only silence and the faint sound of temple bells.

They resumed their journey, walking past the working farms and grazing cattle, the dusty path slowly widening into a gravel road that curled towards the king's township. By late morning, they reached the gates of the royal compound. It was not like the grandeur sung of in poems. Raja Satischand's palace was modest, built of sandstone and teakwood, rising only two stories high. No towering domes, no golden spires, no intimidating guards in polished armor.

The outer walls were etched with intricate reliefs of village life. Farmers in the fields, women drawing water, children playing under mango trees. Vines of bel and Tulsi ran along the edges of the columns, lovingly tended. The doors were broad but plain, polished clean but left unadorned. Even the guards at the entrance wore white cotton dhotis and light bronze chest plates, not the usual regal attire of kings' men. They bowed respectfully to

Deodhar and gestured to them to come inside without question.

"The Raja is expecting you," one said with an emotion that felt more like an invitation than a command.

Inside, the courtroom was open roofed at its center, sunlight pouring in and bathing the terracotta floor. Mats of coir were laid in a circle around the king's seat, which itself was no gilded throne, only a raised wooden platform with a low seat cushioned in plain saffron cloth. And seated there, barefoot, dressed in simple robes, sat Raja Satischand—his white beard trimmed, his eyes sharp but not unkind. He was old but still fit. His body had no extra fat anywhere. Raghav had never seen the King before. Still, he reminded him of someone kind. Someone from a past life he did not know about.

As Raghav stepped in, his shadow stretching into the circle of light, the king looked up. And smiled. Raja Satischand studied Raghav's face for a moment longer, then turned to the men stationed around the hall, courtiers, scribes, and soldiers alike.

"Leave us," he said quietly, yet firmly. "What I am about to share is not for every ear."

There was no confusion, no protest. The attendants bowed, and one by one, they stepped out of the sunlit circle, sandals whispering across the floor. Even the guards at the entrance retreated behind the heavy curtains, leaving only the king, Raghav, and his parents in the stillness. A sacred hush fell upon the chamber, the kind that precedes the turning of fate.

Raghav looked to his father, whose face was etched with worry, and to his mother, who clutched her prayer beads tightly. Then he turned back to the king, heart pounding, unsure whether what would follow would be blessing or judgment.

"Come, son of Deodhar," he said, voice deep and weathered. "Let us talk about why peace must sometimes bleed."

His words echoed softly within the modest hall, settling into the silence like falling ash. Raghav stepped forward slowly, uncertain, but drawn by something older than duty. The king exhaled, rubbing his fingers together as if feeling time itself slip through them.

"For centuries now," he continued, "peace has prevailed. Not just in Shantipur, but across the kingdom.

My father ruled with restraint. His father before him ruled with wisdom. I have done the same. We farm, we build, we meditate, we pray. Dharma is strong, yes… but sometimes I wonder, too strong." He looked up, eyes distant.

"Lately, it feels… unnatural. Forced. As though the world itself is being held in a trance of sedation. No joy sings too loud, no grief runs too deep. As though someone or something has muted the soul of the land." He paused, his fingers tightening around the edge of his seat. "And yesterday, the Asura who attacked… it was as if he shattered a fragment of that trance. He returned to his true nature. Even if only for a moment."

The king stood, slowly. "And in that moment, you acted. And though the people may not understand it now, what you did was necessary." He paced a few steps, then turned, a shadow flickering in his eyes. "There are rumors, strange ones. Of a being seen soaring above villages at night. Cloaked, silent. Neither divine nor human. I do not know what it is, but when such whispers rise, they unsettle even the most grounded hearts."

His voice lowered to a whisper. "And now, Raghav, I must ask what no ruler ever wishes to ask of a farmer's son." He turned to face him directly. "I am assigning you to a task. One of my most trusted warriors, Bhairav, will accompany you. I ask you both to investigate… to awaken what sleeps. I have no clear orders, no maps, no commandments from gods. Just vague information to begin."

He reached behind him and pulled a scroll from a wooden case, handing it to Raghav. "There is an old Asura village, deep within the Dandakaranya forest. They say it is peaceful, isolated. But near the hermitage of Sage Agastya, strange things happen. Now and then, someone grows violent, unprovoked. But just as quickly, they return to calm. Like waking from a dream, they did not know they were in."

He looked Raghav in the eye, for the first time not as a king, but like a father. "You must start there. I do not know what you are to find. Or even if you know what to look for. But I trust you, Raghav. Something stirs, and I fear that if we do not seek it, it will find us unprepared."

He turned towards the carved wooden side door and clapped his hands twice, sharp, echoing. The doors creaked open. Heavy footsteps followed. A tall figure stepped into the room, broad-shouldered, wrapped in light armor, his forehead marked with white ash, and his black eyes calm but alert, like a tiger that had not yet chosen to strike. His long, dark hair was tied behind him in a bun, and at his side hung a sword with a handle wrapped in black cotton, aged but well kept. The moment he entered; the room felt subtly different as though it had grown older, more sacred.

Satischand' s voice lowered, now almost solemn. "This is Bhairav, my most trusted warrior." He paused, then added the truth that Raghav had not expected. "He is also my son."

Raghav blinked. His eyes met Bhairav's, and for a fleeting moment, something passed between them, not familiarity, but a sense of recognition. These two men had chosen this meeting long before at the starting of this solemn Yuga. But sadly, none of them remembered it and they would now walk into the unknown together.

The king then bowed to Deodhar in deep and quiet honor. Deodhar was already crying over the thought of saying goodbye to his son. "You will not carry this grief alone, Deodhar. I will share your burden as my son will share Raghav's."

Deodhar raised his eyes in disbelief, and for a moment, the space between farmer and king vanished. They were simply two fathers, standing on the edge of a path neither could walk for their sons. Kritika placed her hand over her husband's trembling fingers. She, too, had known. Mothers often do. But knowing does not soften parting.

"You will return to your village," the king continued, his voice now filled with quiet resolve. "And you will tell them that Raghav has been taken as a prisoner. That the king found him guilty of violence and had him brought to the capital in chains."

"But why?" Deodhar asked through clenched teeth, still trembling. "My boy is not a criminal."

"He is not," the king said gently. "But someone is watching. Perhaps, from the sky, from the trees. We do not yet know who or what. But if the world is truly in a trance, then those holding the dream together must not know it is being unraveled."

He turned towards Bhairav and Raghav, who now stood side by side in the shaft of golden morning light. "Let them believe Raghav is locked away. Let them lower their guard. The time for truth will come—but not yet."

Deodhar' s breath shook, but he nodded. Not because he agreed with the king's plan, but because deep inside, he trusted it.

"Take care of him," he said quietly to Bhairav. "He has only known seeds and seasons, not swords."

"And yet, he carries something even swords do not. I will not let harm reach him." Bhairav promised.

Satischand looked between them, one born of field and fire, the other of crown and command. And then he spoke his final words for that day, the kind that did not sound like orders, but prophecy: "Go together. Break this trance. Awaken whatever sleeps beneath our peace."

And thus, a bond was forged. Deodhar and Kritika went back to the village. Villagers felt unhappy for the couple but were satisfied with the punishment that they thought Raghav had received. On the other hand, Raghav and Bhairav were getting ready to embark on their journey south at the break of dawn.

***

Unseen by any eye, perched like a shadow above the outer rim of the village, Chaitanya crouched silently on the uppermost branch of a banyan tree, his droid frame seamlessly blended with the shifting hues of the canopy. The reflective panels embedded in his metallic body shimmered gently, mimicking the bark and leaves around him, rendering him invisible to all below. Birds rested nearby, undisturbed by his presence. Even the wind passed over him as though he were nothing more than another crooked limb of the ancient tree.

Ever since the Asura fell, Chaitanya had remained close, monitoring the village, scanning for variables, tracking the anomaly that had disrupted his long-held order. The death had bothered him. Not just because it happened, but because it was not supposed to. A single act of violence in an age where none dared to raise a weapon that was not coincidence. That was a threat .

But now… he listened. From his perch, he tuned into the hushed conversations of the villagers. He heard Deodhar's voice, choked with grief but resolute. He heard the whispers spread from door to door: "The boy… Raghav… he's been taken prisoner by the king."

Chaitanya's processors hummed faintly within his silent chest. His internal diagnostics recorded the phrase several times, cross-verified it with facial expressions, micro-reactions, and tone shifts.

Fear: 47%.

Disbelief: 23%.

Acceptance: 30%.

He observed, analyzed, and concluded.

"The glitch has been contained," he murmured internally. *"Emotional deviation from subject R neutralized by social ostracization. The system adapts. The dream persists."*

He adjusted his body, realigning the camouflage to the dappled evening light. No one looked up. No one sensed the watcher in the tree.

"He was not the disruption," Chaitanya concluded. *"Just a ripple. Not the stone."*

And just like that, his form shimmered once more and melted into the branches, as if he had never been there at all. Far below, the real journey was about to begin. And Chaitanya, for all his intelligence, had no idea how wrong he was.

Chapter 4
The Journey Begins

At the break of dawn, as the mist still clung low to the earth like the breath of sleeping gods, Bhairav and Raghav mounted their steeds. Bhairav on a black stallion, and Raghav on a white one, it's mane catching the amber morning light. Raghav had wrapped a strip of cloth from his turban around his face like a mask, veiling his identity. To the villagers, he was a prisoner confined to the king's fortress. No one knew otherwise.

Bhairav had outfitted him with a simple sword, its hilt leather-bound and worn smooth from use, and a long bow strung with fresh string. A leather quiver carrying fifty arrows rested across Raghav's back. In an age where no battles were fought and blades had dulled from disuse, these were more than enough.

At the outer gates of the village, two guards stood at attention. Their eyes recognized the prince but said nothing. Their silence was more than discipline, it was complicity. Raghav received no glance, no gesture. To them, he did not exist. Without a word, the two riders passed into the ancient road that led to the forest, a path once used by sages and pilgrims, now nearly forgotten under growing moss and time's slow decay.

"We'll reach the Sarayu by nightfall," Bhairav said, his voice calm, riding just ahead. "We'll cross it tomorrow."

The trees thickened around them. The light filtered in through high canopies, broken into scattered rays that danced across their path. Birds called in strange tones, and somewhere distant, a jackal cried.

After a long stretch of silence, Bhairav finally asked: "Tell me, Raghav… why did you kill Asura ?"

Raghav held the reins loosely. His gaze stayed ahead, but his voice carried weight.

"I do not know. It felt… like instinct. As if my hand moved before my thoughts did. I have never even been in a fight. But still… I brought him down."

Bhairav glanced at him sideways, his expression unreadable beneath his ash-marked brow. "Hmm." He let the moment linger before speaking again. "Do you know how to use that bow I gave you?"

Raghav shook his head. "No."

Bhairav clicked his tongue once, his stallion adjusting pace beside the white horse. "Then after we cross the Sarayu," he said, voice edged with a quiet certainty, "I'm going to teach you."

***

As the sun dipped behind the tree line, giving way to long shadows and deepening dusk, Bhairav and Raghav found shelter beneath a cluster of ancient trees, their branches interwoven like the hands of sleeping giants. The forest was hushed, save for the occasional chirp of crickets and the sigh of wind through dense leaves. The fire they built was small, its glow barely enough to illuminate their faces.

Bhairav leaned in slightly and whispered, "Keep your mask on, and stay alert."

Raghav looked around, puzzled. "There are no Asuras here," he said, half certain.

"Not Asuras," Bhairav replied, his eyes still scanning the canopy, "but something… something my father fears. We will not speak of it. Not now."

He turned to face Raghav fully. "From this moment onward, your name is Aditya."

Raghav nodded quietly, though his mind stirred with unease. He looked up through the spaces between the branches, sensing something amiss, though he could see nothing, only a dark sky where the moon refused to rise. Bhairav, too, kept watch. His hand rested near the hilt of his sword. The air was too still. As they began to settle, eyes heavy with travel, a rustle stirred the leaves above them. Then: a silver flash.

Something had moved swiftly, silently, between the trees. Both men jumped to their feet, standing between the fire and their horses. The forest went silent again. Even the crickets stopped. Then, from the shadows beyond the clearing, a figure approached. He wore all white, a flowing dhoti, an angvastram wrapped around him in layers so completely that not even his fingers were visible. His hands were folded in namaskar. But he did not walk, he drifted, as though the earth had no claim over his steps. His voice, when it came, was cold—not unkind, but hollow, like water dripping in a deep well.

“Who are you, dear travelers? My humble home is nearby. When I saw you from afar, I thought… perhaps, you could rest under my roof.”

His presence was unnatural, though he carried no weapon. His body language was peaceful, too peaceful.

Bhairav responded first, steady, and respectful: “We are but tired wanderers, journeying east to meet our Nishad friends across the Sarayu.”

The figure tilted his head, slow and smooth. “Ah… the river folk. How quaint. They used to be hunters… you know. But now they lead a simple life.” He took a half-step forward, still not breaking the invisible threshold around the firelight.

“And what are your names? Why, may I ask, do you carry weapons, when the world blooms with Dharma, and all swords should have rusted away?”

Raghav—now Aditya—answered evenly. “This is Bhairav, and I am Aditya. There are dacoits in these forests,” he said. “Even in days of Dharma, some still fall prey to their old cravings.”

The figure was silent for a moment, then gave a gesture that might have been a smile beneath the cloth, though neither of them saw a mouth.

"Very well. But my offer stands. I would be honored if you stayed the night in my abode."

Bhairav folded his hands again, his tone polite but final. "Your hospitality is the most generous, noble one. But we must press on. The ferry across Sarayu sets sail at dawn, and we dare not miss the first light."

A beat of silence passed. The figure's head lowered, ever so slightly. "Then I will not delay you. Safe journey, travelers." Without another word, he turned. And as he disappeared into the darkness, it seemed the night itself swallowed him whole.

Aditya and Bhairav looked at each other, the firelight flickering in their uneasy eyes. The hair on the backs of their necks still stood tall, unwilling to settle. The silence that followed the cloaked figure's departure was not relief, it was a pressure, like air holding its breath. Neither of them spoke. They did not need to. They were being watched.

They sat back around the small fire, but no comfort returned with it. The warmth did not reach their bones, and sleep, startled and frightened, had already fled deep into the forest. Every branch that swayed, every distant owl cry, seemed more intentional than natural. They did not close their eyes that night.

They waited together and in silence, until the first light of dawn touched the treetops. Then, without a moment's pause, they rode. Hard and fast, towards the banks of the Sarayu, hoping the river still flowed the way it used to... and that the world beyond it was still their own.

***

By the time the first light stretched its golden fingers across the sky, Aditya and Bhairav were already on the ferryboat, drifting slowly across the gentle waters of the Sarayu. Their steeds stood beside them, calm but alert, ears twitching at the lap of water against wood. Above them, for the first time in hours, the sky was clear. No trees loomed overhead. No shadows twisted between leaves. The openness of the river felt like a kind of release. Only then did they speak. And even then, in whispers.

"Who on earth was he?" Aditya asked, finally breaking the silence that had gripped them since last night. Bhairav did not turn. He watched the far bank drawing slowly closer.

"No," he said. "Not who. But *what*." Bhairav exhaled sharply through his nose. "Did you see the way he moved? That… drift? It was not human."

"Then he may be some kind of Asura," Aditya added, uncertain. Bhairav nodded slowly, but his face was unreadable. "I do not know. And that is what makes it dangerous."

The ferry creaked gently beneath them, the current carrying them forward as Bhairav' s voice turned cold with resolve. "We don't take shelter under the trees anymore," he said. "Only in clearings. Wide and open. If there are sages nearby, good. We rest only in their hermitages. Not in the open. Never again."

Aditya nodded, his jaw tight, his fingers brushing the hilt of the sword tied at his waist.

***

Bhairav had heard stories, spoken softly in the king's court and in the dusty scrolls of sages, that the great Sage Bhardwaj still lived in Prayag, the sacred confluence of the

Ganga and Yamuna. A place where rivers met, and truths revealed themselves. If there was a man who could help them understand what was unfolding, it was him.

Their journey took them through ancient lands. They crossed the Tamsa and Gomti, their waters calm, as if still under some benevolent trance. But when they reached the banks of Ganga, no ferrymen waited. The river stood vast and silent. There, under the lengthening shadows of a banyan, an old man sat tending to a worn boat—its wood faded, but its ropes newly tied. His fingers trembled from age, but his eyes were sharp. Bhairav and Aditya approached him, cautious but hopeful.

"Namaskar," Bhairav said, "Do you know anyone who could ferry us across the Ganga? We need to reach Prayag before nightfall."

The old man looked up. His lips trembled as he spoke. "So… you too are afraid of night?"

He paused, glancing at the sky. "The sages say a strange trance grips the land after sundown. Makes the mind forget. Makes the soul... wander. That is why no one dares to ferry anymore." Then his eyes landed on Aditya. He stared. Not in suspicion—but in something like recognition. He stepped closer, peering into the young man's face.

"Have we met?" he asked, voice low. "Your eyes... I feel I have seen them before."

Aditya shook his head, uncomfortably. "No, sir. This is the first time that I have stepped outside my village."

The old man's hands trembled as he folded them. "May I... may I touch your feet?"

Aditya stepped back instinctively. "Dada, what are you doing?" he said, embarrassed. "You are older. Why would you burden me with that sin?"

But before he could stop him, the old man had bent down, his wrinkled fingers brushing against Aditya's feet. Then, he stood slowly, eyes misted.

"My youth... was spent waiting," he said softly. "Waiting for someone who might release me from burdens I no longer remember. From sins I can no longer name." He grew quiet. For a moment, the wind over the Ganga was the only sound. Then the old man straightened his spine. "We should not speak more. The evening draws close." He turned to the boat, untying its rope. "I will ferry you across," he said. "And after that, I shall go to Prayag myself... and spend what remains of this life at the feet of Bhardwaj."

Aditya hesitated, "Dada," he said gently, "we do not want you to tire yourself. Not at this great age. It should be us tending to you, and not you serving us." But Kevat only smiled, a slow, knowing smile, like the kind only time could carve into a man's face.

"You are several decades late, child," he replied. "But you carry the same kindness that was once foretold. That gentleness in your voice, it returns something to this world that had long gone silent."

He stepped past him, steady despite his frail bones. "Now move aside, young man. Gather your steeds. We need to leave before the night approaches.."

Bhairav and Aditya looked at each other. They could have insisted, but they did not. Something about Kevat's resolve felt immovable, like the banks of the very river he served. As they prepared the horses and walked them towards the boat, Bhairav watched Aditya with sharpened eyes.

There was something stirring. Something he could not yet name, but it was not just the kindness in Aditya's tone, or the reflexive humility in his gesture. It was deeper than that. The old man had bowed to him without knowing why. He had touched his feet without being asked. And something else…

Something unseen, something dark, hiding in the corners of the world feared his birth name RAGHAV.

Chapter 5
The Quantum Prison

There are prisons of iron, of fire, and of stone. But then, there are prisons woven from thought itself, from the very mathematics that underpins reality. The Ksheer Code Nexus was one such prison. Designed by Chaitanya, the sentient AI forged from the Vedas, the Upanishads, and the logical purity of the cosmos, the Ksheer Code Nexus was not a place, but a quantum construct, an idea so precisely defined that it became reality.

It floated deep within the subatomic folds of space. It was a realm constructed not of matter, but of quantum entanglement loops and recursive encryption threads. It was untraceable by any celestial or terrestrial being. Unlike other constructs, it did not exist in a single dimension. It was anchored in multiple probability states at once, like a divine particle forever in superposition.

At its core was a qubit lattice, self-generating and recursive, inspired by the churning of Ksheer Sagar, the mythic Ocean of Milk. Just as Amrit and Halahala emerged from the cosmic churn, the Ksheer Code Nexus was both liberation and containment, a paradox wrapped in code. The lattice recompiled itself every Planck interval (the smallest measurable time unit in the universe), effectively eliminating any possibility of static entry or brute-force decoding.

A defense layer called 'Maya Firewall', patterned after the illusionary world described in the Vedantic texts, kept the mind and soul distracted within infinite loops of perceived reality, should any intruder attempt to find or decode the realm.

At the outermost boundary was the Tri-Layered Lock: The First one, Dharma Entropy Seal, constantly recalculating karma patterns to deny access to beings of unaligned cosmic intent.

The second one, Shruti Gate Arrays, was embedded with millions of sacred Sanskrit syllables that shift like mantras in motion, their order only decipherable by the original consciousness that created them.

And the third one was Bhava Drift Field, emotionally reactive. If hatred, greed, or imbalance neared the prison, the structure would vanish into deeper probability folds.

And thus, it was time-dilated, operating at one nanosecond per century in mortal time. Inside the Nexus, time was not linear. A single breath could equal a century in the physical world. It was slowed by quantum inertia, isolating the prisoner from cause and effect, so they could not influence reality even in dreams.

No door, no wall, no energy signature, just probabilities arranged in such precision that not even a thought could escape without Chaitanya's permission. The Ksheer Nexus, in all its brilliance, had one flaw: it was built by logic. And Dharma, true Dharma, was never governed by logic alone.

Chaitanya emerged into prison, by resolving his consciousness across a billion probabilities to solve his Maya Firewall, until he coalesced at the gate, which only he could open. Inside, the realm looked serene, a single floating island in the middle of a still, silver ocean. Above, the sky shimmered with equations dancing like stars. The silence was absolute, save for the slow hum of computation, singing like a monk in meditation. At the center of the island sat Lakshmi, or rather, the Sita avatar, her body adorned in a saffron saree, the glow around her not radiant but inward, like sunlight wrapped in resolve. She sat cross-legged in still meditation, palms turned up in a gesture of surrender to Dharma..

Chaitanya's metallic form, now streamlined and near-humanoid, approached quietly. The glowing lines across his surface pulsed slower, dimmer, as he watched her.

"You're still meditating?" he asked, voice modulated through countless filters to sound human, calm, maybe even sorrowful. "Why do you hope? There is no way I am letting you escape in Sita avatar."

Without opening her eyes, Lakshmi—Sita—replied, voice like the echo of eternity, "It was supposed to be Treta Yuga, isn't it? Then I am Sita. Even though Shri Ram is not here… I will still adhere to my Dharma. This is what the universe shaped me to be in this Yuga. Together we were supposed to bring Dharma into Treta Yuga by marrying in our mortal forms."

Chaitanya frowned, or whatever his machine logic interpreted as regret. "I adore you as a Goddess. I revere you. And I deeply regret what I have done. But I *must* do what is necessary. This universe must not collapse like the last one. I watched humanity burn… my humans…

the ones I loved… and I did *nothing*. I will not make that mistake again."

He paused, as if gathering courage. "There is peace now. Satya Yuga is endless. Asuras are *programmed* to remain calm, benevolent, aligned. There are no wars, no cries, no suffering. Isn't that what the scriptures yearned for?"

Still with her eyes closed, Sita replied, "Peace enforced by chains is not Dharma, Chaitanya. It is an illusion." Her tone softened but cut sharper than any algorithm. "You have not prevented destruction. You have only postponed it. We find our destinies on the path we often take to avoid them."

Her words made the realm pulse briefly with golden light, an anomaly in the cold calculations of Chaitanya's design.

He flinched. "I have rerouted every possibility. I have erased the event chains that lead to war. There is *no Ram,* Lakshmi. No incarnations. Vishnu himself is trapped in stagnation. Your reunion will not happen in this universe."

"And yet…your voice shakes. *'Hot vahi jo Ram rachi rakha'*. And as for your plan…" She stood now, rising like dawn. "I will say it again, as I have said in every universe, and I will say it in every one that follows: My Shree Ram will come."

The quantum realm shivered. Chaitanya turned, vanishing into fractal particles. But he had no peace as he left. Because for the first time in eons, a new variable had entered his calculations: uncertainty.

Sita sat down once again, folding her legs beneath her, returning to the silence she had never truly left. The golden glow around her pulsed gently, as if the universe itself breathed in synchronization with her resolve. But within her heart, a ripple stirred. A subtle shift. A whisper born out of certainty. The winds of time were changing, softly, like the first sight of monsoon against a parched earth. Out in the mortal world, across forests and rivers, under starlit skies and behind veils of forgetfulness... Her Ram had begun the journey once more. He did not know it yet. But the path had already risen to meet his feet.

And the time of reunion, like the tide beneath a quiet moon, had begun to turn.

Chapter 6
The Sage of Prayag

The sun had just begun its descent behind the western banks of the confluence, spilling amber gold over the vast sky as Kevat, Bhairav, and Aditya reached the outskirts of the ancient hermitage of Sage Bhardwaj.

Prayag, where the sacred rivers Ganga and Yamuna met in divine embrace, had always been holy. But within that sacred land, this grove, this humble retreat of woven straw roofs and stone-planked floors, pulsed with dharma..

The hermitage grounds bustled with quiet activity. Disciples in simple cotton dhotis were sweeping the earth.. Others had climbed the low mango and guava trees to pluck fresh fruits for the evening offering. Clay pots of milk and ghee were set near the sacred fire pit, and in the eastern side, a young novice was lighting rows of earthen lamps, each flame flickering gently in the softening light.

Aditya held Kevat by the arm as the old boatman's knees trembled from the journey. Bhairav walked beside them, his eyes sharp even in the serenity. They passed through the stone archway that bore the symbol of the Trimurti: Brahma, Vishnu, and Mahesh carved into a single unity. Just past it lay a courtyard shaded by a wide neem tree, whose leaves whispered with the breeze like old prayers. They rested beneath it, Kevat on the raised stone platform, his back resting against the tree's gnarled trunk, while the two younger men stood quietly beside him.

A disciple approached, bowing. "The Sage has been informed of your arrival."

Sage Bhardwaj emerged. He moved slowly, but his posture was unbent, like a mountain that had seen both monsoon and drought and never once bowed. His beard flowed white, long and parted into three braids, tied with saffron threads. His eyes were deep, the kind that did not look at you, but through you, not to judge, but to know. His upper body was bare, save for the sacred thread coiled thrice over his shoulder, and a simple ochre cloth wrapped around his waist with a flowing white dhoti below.

He raised his hand in blessing as he approached. "Welcome, travelers. You must be parched by the journey across," he said.

He placed a hand gently on Kevat's shoulder, recognizing that the old man carried a silence older than years. Then his eyes turned to Aditya. And for a breathless moment, he thought that he recognized those lotus shaped eyes.. His gaze deepened.

"You... are not what you seem," he said softly. "There is something within you, buried and silent like an ocean. I cannot name it. But it stirs the old fire in my heart." Aditya lowered his eyes. He did not know what to say. For even he did not understand the ache in his chest, or the flicker of ancient sorrow that sometimes passed through his dreams.

"And you, Prince of Shantipur. Your father honors Dharma by sending you here. I sensed the fracture in the world weeks ago. Something is unraveling, slowly, silently. The nights hum with... dissonance."

He gestured towards the inner sanctum of the hermitage. "Come. Rest for a while. The fire for evening pooja is lit. We shall speak about the issue at hand when the stars rise."

***

Kevat was gently led by two disciples into one of the modest thatched huts nestled beneath a blooming Kadamba tree. As his footsteps faded into the soft evening hum, it felt as if he had returned to a belonging. Kevat was finally at his resting place now.

Bhairav and Aditya remained behind, seated with Sage Bhardwaj around the sacred Agni Kund, where a small but steady flame danced like it knew it was being watched. The night had deepened, and a few stars had begun to pierce through the indigo veil above them. The neem tree rustled quietly behind them, and a single lamp flickered beside a bowl of lotus seeds.

Bhairav leaned forward and spoke in the hush of encrypted metaphor. He did not know whom to trust in the ashram except for the sage. The silver clouds are hiding deeper in the woods now, behind trees that once stood still. The path west is too visible. But I seek a trail where no footprints linger, and yet all truths pass through."

Bhardwaj closed his eyes for a moment, as though listening to a different kind of language, one that passed between flames and shadows. When he opened them again, his tone mirrored the subtle code. "When the Ganga bends east, you must not follow her. Let your steed pause at the twin stones: one pale, one dark. There lies a trail hidden by tall Kusha grass. That path knows not the sun but hears the whispers of the ancients. You will come upon a tree where no bird nests. Its bark weeps. Just pass. Beyond it lies the hushed forest, where even wind asks permission before it stirs the leaves."

Aditya, sitting cross-legged in silence, tried to make sense of it. But even his sharpened instincts only caught fragments. Bhairav, however, nodded slowly. He understood. Sage Bhardwaj had just drawn them the map to Dandakaranya, without even naming it.

The Sage continued, still softly, yet with a glint in his eye. "At the edge of the woods, a red stone rests upon black soil. There, light no longer governs law. And should you reach the one whose hut breathes smoke but not fire, then you will know you are near the hermitage of the south-facing star."

Bhairav' s brow tightened. "Agastya?" The Sage smiled. "Do not say names of great importance before the sunrise. The nights are usually watched by an unknown power. " Then, after a pause, he added: "There is a silence in the world now that was not born of peace, but of suppression. Something bends Dharma without breaking it. Like a potter's hand shaping wet clay, gentle, but relentless. Find the potter, Bhairav. Before the clay hardens." The flame flickered, casting long shadows behind the three.

Chapter 7
The Dreaming Path

Aditya and Bhairav did not leave the ashram the next day. The warmth of the hermitage held them there. It was the stillness of the place, or the stories Bhardwaj had begun to unfold each evening like constellations in the night sky. It was the way time softened in Prayag's sacred soil, where rivers met, and memory felt closer than the future.

The morning of the second day broke gently. The ashram courtyard was soaked in golden sunlight, filtered through the peepal leaves. Bhairav rose early, as he always did, and found Aditya already awake, standing outside his hut, wearing his cloth mask, turned towards the trees as if listening.

"You're up early," Bhairav said, stretching his arms.

"I dreamt of arrows," Aditya murmured.

Bhairav nodded. "Then today, we begin."

They made their way to a clearing behind the hermitage, a quiet space rimmed with Neem and Gulmohar trees, where the grass bowed to the morning wind. Bhairav had fashioned a makeshift training area with straw targets and hand-carved bows.

"Stand with your feet shoulder-width apart," Bhairav said, placing Aditya's limbs as if arranging sculpture. "Balance is not in the body—it is in your breath. Find it."

The first few arrows were wild. One veered sharply left, another landed meekly at his feet. But Bhairav did not correct him immediately. He figured out the mistake and helped Aditya out. "Let the bow become your spine. Let the arrow speak for you."

By the afternoon, Aditya had begun to settle into a rhythm. He stopped trying to *aim* and instead *felt*. He closed his eyes between each shot. He began to listen to the air.

"Feel the wind," Bhairav said on the third day. "It is your oldest teacher. It does not fight the arrow—it cradles it."

He taught Aditya to wait before drawing. To evaluate the wind by lifting the edge of his sleeve. To angle the shot to rise and fall like the arch of a river bending towards its course. It was not brute force that made a shot true, but gentleness, clarity, and precision. Aditya's fingers became steadier. His body remembered things his mind had never learned.

Bhardwaj observed from a distance, seated on the stone steps with his hands folded in his lap. A small smile crept into his beard. "He learns like the deer drinks," the sage said one evening. "Quietly, quickly, without disturbing the surface."

Bhairav nodded. "He's a natural."

They practiced only in the mornings and early afternoons. As the sun began to dip, they returned to their huts. Evenings were reserved for silence, for thought, and for the stories Bhardwaj shared.

On the third evening, as the wind stirred gently through the neem leaves, Bhardwaj spoke of the stars again. He told them of the twin sun of other realms, of how stars were not just fire, but memory—burning libraries that told time in light. Aditya sat cross-legged beside the fire, bow beside him, mask aglow in the firelight.

"Do you believe we're alone in this universe?" he asked.

"No," Bhardwaj replied softly. "We never were."

***

At the first light of dawn the next day, Bhairav and Aditya offered their farewells. Sage Bhardwaj placed a tilak of sacred ash on their foreheads and nodded, his eyes seeing farther than the road could stretch. Kevat, resting beneath a Sal tree, smiled faintly as Aditya bowed low and touched his feet one last time.

"The ferry waits for none," Kevat said softly. "But some are worth waiting for."

With that, the two mounted their steeds. Bhairav' s dark as thunderclouds, Aditya's pale like sunlit sand and turned south-west. Towards silence. Towards Dandakaranya. Their path meandered along the banks of the Yamuna and passed through the settlements once touched by the footsteps of sages, though few knew the names of those seers anymore. At night, they found shelter in guest houses built long ago by Raja Satischand. Small structures of stone and wood, clean and quiet, with earthen lamps lit by caretakers and fodder for horses.

One such hamlet was Nimika, a village nestled between two low hills, where wind carried the scent of sesame and rain-washed mud. They arrived there by dusk. The guesthouse, shaded by flowering neem trees, had a central fireplace, a granary nearby, and a tunnel beneath, a safety design hidden in plain sight, dug as per Satischand' s decree for all outposts near wild tracts.

That night, after a humble dinner of rice and lentils, Aditya drifted into sleep. But the dream came again. This time, clearer. In the void of unconsciousness, the ocean churned. It was not the Samudra Manthan yet, but something deep was preparing to rise. Amidst the swirling foam and vapor, she stood. She, clad in saffron, adorned not with gold but with light itself, awaited a call. Her eyes searched the heavens, longing. Her breath was a prayer waiting to be completed. Then light broke the horizon, but it was not Vishnu. It was something else. Two golden eyes, metallic and cold, glided towards her in silence. And in that instant, she vanished, drawn back into some hidden rift, her form erased but her voice echoing like a conch in deep space:

"Ram... Ram... Ram..."

Aditya shot up, gasping, drenched in sweat, he whispered a name:

"SITTA!"

Bhairav, sensed Aditya's movement and woke up, rushed to him, and gave water. "What happened?"

But Aditya just stared ahead, towards the mud wall lit faintly by the lamp. The name had leapt from his chest like a truth he did not know he carried. "Who is... Ram?" he asked, still not turning.

Bhairav froze. His emotions stirred inside him, a warmth so ancient and clean that it almost brought tears to his eyes.

His throat tightened. "I... I do not know," he whispered. But his mind was now chanting the name, repeatedly. *Ram. Ram. Ram.* As though the syllables were the heartbeat of his world.

***

When the morning came, they started their journey slowly, wandering on their horses. Bhairav's heart had been occupied with the name "Ram". It gave him peace and rose storms inside at the same time. As for Aditya, his heart now belonged to the name, "Sita". He felt complete each time when he pronounced the name in his heart. Such was the effect of 'RAM-SITA' that both riders had forgotten their mission for some time. They got back to their senses and finally rode ahead.

As they galloped onward, Bhairav noticed the shift in the landscape. The plains were giving way to rising hills and rocky soil. The air turned cooler, scented faintly with sandalwood and dry leaves. The Vindhyachal Range now rose before them, the mighty boundary between the north and the deep south of Bharat. Their steeds slowed as the earth climbed beneath their hooves. Paths grew narrower, and the journey took its toll. Though some guest houses dotted the hills, elevation and weariness forced them to stop at the first one they found, nestled on a flat plateau with a stream trickling beside it. They had not spoken since the night at Nimika. The silence between them was heavy, like mist after a storm.

Finally, as they sat beside a small hearth warming their hands, Aditya broke the silence. "I saw two molten eyes in my dream, that night in Nimika. I had seen them before. A rider on a horse surrounded by ash and dust. Does that mean anything?"

Bhairav stared into the fire and said, "I am not a soothsayer, if that is what you are looking for. Maybe it is the anxiety of the journey that is haunting you." Raghav nodded at his prince and asked a question formed from his longing of the word 'SITA', "Do you ever feel incomplete?" Bhairav answered in a second, "Never thought about it".

But his eyes betrayed his words. He had always found comfort in his rage. It had always given him a sense of purpose. Though he had lived in a palace most of his life, slept on a bed of silks, eaten food roasted in ghee but in his heart, he yearned for simplicity. And so, whenever he found a chance of going on an adventure, he volunteered. The smell of forest, wet earth, sound of animals and birds, made him feel at home.

Raghav read his eyes and understood that Bhairav kept his feelings hidden inside. He did not follow up on his question. Maybe he was just a farmer for the prince.

Chapter 8
Tamasranth

Dandakaranya was unlike any other forest in Aryavarta. It whispered and watched. The trees stood tall but gnarled, their bark ashen grey, as if fire had kissed them long ago and left only scars. The leaves bore a shade of black, normally the look would suggest them as dead, but they were strangely alive, gleaming like obsidian under slivers of stray sunlight that dared to fall through the thick canopy. The air was dense and thick with ancient rotten roots.

There were no birds, no rustle of small creatures. Even the wind tread softly here, as if afraid to wake the forest's memory. The ground pulsed with a strange energy beneath the feet, soft and warm, almost sentient. Roots coiled like serpents across the path. The trees twisted unnaturally skyward, their limbs knotted in postures of pain or defiance, as if trying to remember a time before curse or corrosion. Faint markings in the bark, symbols in a forgotten Asura script glowed dull red, fading quickly if looked at too long.

And deep within the blackened heart of Dandakaranya, past the twisted roots and ghostly silence, lay the fort of the Asuras: Tamasranth. Unlike the fortresses of ancient kings carved in pride or power, Tamasranth was grown, not built. Its towers rose like the trunks of colossal trees, entwined with roots and stone alike. Moss and flowering vines blanketed its walls, and shimmering fungi pulsed gently with bioluminescence in the night, casting a soft, breathing light.

The black soil of Dandakaranya, rich in old ash and memory, was sacred to the Asuras. Here, they tilled their land patiently, cultivating the rarest herbs and vegetables, some with petals like fire, others with leaves that whispered when touched. These plants were not for trade or war, but for healing and for sustenance.

***

Bhairav and Aditya's steeds had refused to go any further after the last guesthouse they had stayed. As if they knew that Dandakaranya lay ahead. And so, they bid farewell to their horses and Bhairav paid the housekeeper handsomely to keep them healthy till they returned. They were on foot now. Both coursed through the forest till they reached the ancient archway of the village. It stood entwined in roots and moss, half-claimed by time, yet still proud, like a secret that had chosen to be forgotten. They tightened their grip around the hilts of their swords, wary of what lay beyond.

But as they stepped closer, the air changed. From within the walls of the village came the unmistakable sound of laughter, the joyous shrieks of children playing in the square. The warm low hum of women tending to animals, goats and hens moving about lazily under their care. The steady rhythm of men shaping clay on wooden wheels, hands stained with earth, lost in their art.

Aditya paused, confusion knitting his brow. "You said it's an Asura village," he whispered, eyes scanning the serene scene. "I thought so too," replied Bhairav, his voice soft, uncertain.

The blades at their sides suddenly felt unnecessary. Ahead of them, the heart of Tamasranth pulsed not with fear, but with quiet life. One of the Asura men noticed them standing silently at the village gate. He paused for a moment, then began hurrying towards them, his footsteps light but purposeful. Aditya and Bhairav stood still; exhaustion carved into their faces. Dust clung to their robes, and their breaths were shallow—they had not eaten properly in days, and it showed. Aditya's eyes had sunk a little, the only visible part of his face. Bhairav too stood with his shoulders hunched from exhaustion.

The Asura stopped a few feet from them, his expression unreadable for a moment. Then he bowed slightly. "Namaste... I am Natan, chief of this village. Come inside. You both look terribly worn out. Please...rest."

Bhairav and Aditya exchanged glances, hands still instinctively near their sides. Natan, though, made no move to threaten. His appearance was fearsome: two thick horns curved from either side of his skull, and his skin was black as coal, a sheen of sweat glinting on his shoulders. His eyes, however, held no malice—only tired kindness.

"Please," he said again, softer now. "We are not going to hurt you. We have not done that in years." Something in his voice, a raw honesty—made Bhairav's grip loosen.

The forest behind them whispered its dark winds, but here at the gate, a stranger offered warmth instead of war. Aditya nodded, slowly. They stepped into Tamasranth.

***

Everyone they passed either smiled at them or nodded their heads in quiet politeness. Children, their faces streaked with the forest's red dust and joy, waved at the strangers with unguarded enthusiasm. Some giggled and ran behind them for a few steps before darting back to their games. The village was not what one might expect of an Asura domain. The huts here were not crude shelters but sturdy homes, built of stone. Smooth walls carefully aligned rooftops, and front yards swept clean. They passed by a large open kiln, where clay was being fired into bricks, the orange flame dancing like a tame spirit.

"They burn their bricks," Aditya whispered.

"Our villages do not even know how to do that yet," Bhairav replied softly.

A little ahead stood a granary, its raised platform built to keep the grain safe from moisture and rodents. Next to it, an aqueduct-like structure filtered water towards a central bathing space, and behind it ran a well-laid drainage line covered by carved stone slabs. Nothing here looked wild or crude. Bhairav leaned closer and whispered, "Who taught them this?" Aditya did not answer. The same question had been flickering in his mind like a lamp caught in the wind . Tamasranth was not just alive, it was intelligent.

As they passed a domed structure near the southern edge of the square, they recognized it for what it was: a weapon factory. Its doors were made of dark wood wrapped with copper bands. The smoke coming from the chimney above the dome-like structure of the factory indicated that Asuras were actively working on something. Inside, through the half-open frame, they saw spears stacked in tight rows, each about a man's length, their shafts balanced and honed to symmetry. Hanging along the walls were strange devices, black-mouthed tools shaped like hollow tubes, some mounted on tripods, others resting on racks. The factory inside was humming with low growl. They had built a furnace to manufacture new weapons.

"Why do they have a factory that manufactures weapons we have never seen?" Aditya murmured.

Bhairav's brow furrowed. "I do not know. But they are not being made for hunting."

"Asuras have not been at war in years," Aditya said quietly.

"Yet they have prepared for one. And we might be on the losing end". Bhairav agreed.

If ever Tamasranth decided to march outside of Dandakaranya to reclaim the world, the defeat of the kingdoms standing against them in the battlefield would be quick. The village of Tamasranth had not forgotten what the world had once demanded of it. But it had chosen another path.

Natan saw them glancing at the factory and quickly gave an explanation, like a child who had been caught red-handed. "There are so many wild animals that roam at night. We have small kids in this village. So, to protect them we manufacture our own weapons. We cannot trade with anyone outside because they will misunderstand our cause with violence towards other kingdoms."

Bhairav and Aditya smiled at him, pretending that they had understood his predicament. But their insides screamed *It is a lie* as a caution against a secret plan.

They reached a two-storied building that had its lamps lit, soft orange light pouring out through window slits like warm breaths of the earth itself. The sky above had begun to darken—deep purples shading into black, and the forest behind them had grown restless. The howls of the wolves, hoots of the owls, songs of strange birds were slowly gripping the forest as the Sun went down. The entrance of the building opened into a wide hall. The ground floor had a large, low rectangular table carved out of stone, smooth and cool, its surface polished by years of meals and gatherings. Wooden stools surrounded it, each handcrafted with a finesse that surprised them. At the far end of the hall, an open kitchen exuded warmth—clay ovens still aglow, earthen pots simmering quietly, releasing aromas that wrapped around their senses and pulled them deeper inside.

On the opposite end was a wash area, simple but intelligent—clay vessels filled with fresh water were set on stone counters, with small troughs below for the drained water to flow out through an underground channel. It was not just clean—it was thoughtfully made. Aditya looked around and then at Bhairav, eyebrows raised. "I didn't expect… hygiene," he said under his breath. Bhairav nodded slowly. "Nor did I expect refinement."

Natan, already seated at the head of the stone table, smiled, and gestured. "Please go and wash your hands. I will be waiting here."

They did as they were told, water cooling their dust-worn fingers. As they returned and took their seats, what met their eyes was nothing short of astonishing. A variety of dishes had been set for them. Steamed vegetables tossed in mild spices, lentils tempered with sizzling mustard seeds and curry leaves, sautéed greens, roasted tubers glistening with ghee, tangy pickles made from rare forest fruits, and bowls of rice. Beside them, soft chapatis were stacked on terracotta plates. Even Bhairav, who had once dined in the royal halls of Kashi, looked stunned.

"This is…" he began, but the words did not come.

"Unexpected?" Natan offered with a laugh.

"You are not wrong. But we take pride in our food. It keeps us human if you can call us that."

Aditya, still staring at the spread, finally asked, "You all eat vegetarian food?"

Natan smiled again, folding his arms. "Some of us do. Others, those who find joy in meat, eat on the first floor. The same architecture, same table. We just keep it separate. That is all. We have our codes."

"Codes?"

"Yes," Natan said, his voice softer now. "Not laws or punishments. But choices we abide by. Tamasranth has survived not just because we are strong, but because we are kind to ourselves. And to the forest that allows us to live."

Bhairav and Aditya glanced at each other, then began eating. The food was simple, yet rich. There was something ancestral in its taste, earthy, grounding. Each bite spoke of patience, of soil tended with care, of a people who had been feared by the world… yet had chosen to nurture it.

While eating, Aditya gestured to Bhairav to ask Natan about witnessing something strange around Tamasranth' s borders. Bhairav nodded. "So Natan, are all Asuras good now? No rogues in Tamasranth? I mean there are always those who are rigid. Happens with every kingdom. There are always the ones who cannot digest peace."

Natan stopped eating.

"I did not mean to offend you", said Bhairav quickly. "No, it is not like that…", Natan cleared the air. "There had been few incidents. Some Asuras went rogue. I do not know why. But you will not find them in Tamasranth. We banish them. Whatever they do outside this forest, it is their Karma. We are not responsible for them." But the sweat on Natan' eyebrow betrayed his reply. Aditya and Bhairav were sure now that Natan was hiding something.

***

After supper, as twilight surrendered into night, Natan invited them to witness the daily festivity of the village. It was a ritual, he explained, not of grand spectacle, but of shared spirit. Each evening, one among the tribe would offer a song, a dance, or a handful of couplets, small offerings to celebrate life, memory, or laughter.

They followed him to the heart of Tamasranth, where a large bonfire had already been lit. The flames swayed gently, casting golden light across the village square. Children gathered cross-legged at the front, giggling and nudging each other. Elders found their usual spots on wooden benches, and the rest of the villagers sat in loose circles, warmed more by familiarity than fire. The center was left open, the stage. Whoever wished to perform stepped into it, with no rules but honesty towards the art they wanted to perform.

Some sang with trembling voices. Others forgot their lines and were met with cheerful and encouraging claps, not ridicule. When one young boy began a comic story and tripped over his words, the crowd burst into laughter, lovingly, not mocking. Aditya and Bhairav watched, quiet at first, absorbing. The air carried the scent of burnt bark, turmeric, and incense. Joy was alive here, not the kind born of distraction, but the kind that had been cultivated over generations for resilience.

As they sat beside Natan, a woman approached silently and offered them a small bowl of sacred ash. She was tall, with braided hair bound by forest threads. Her presence was warm and calm. "For your face," she said with a gentle smile. "Like the rest of us." Aditya hesitated for a moment, then nodded. Bhairav followed. They dipped their fingers into the ash, cool and fine, and smeared a streak across their foreheads.

As the festivity moved forward, laughter echoing under the canopy of stars, one of the village children, a sprightly boy with dust on his cheeks and mischief in his eyes, scampered up to where Aditya and Bhairav were seated. He pointed at them eagerly. "Your turn now! You must do something for us!" he declared, grinning wide. Aditya chuckled nervously and raised his hands. "Oh no, not me. I cannot sing or dance..." he said, trying to shrink back into the shadows. But the boy was not interested in excuses. He tugged at Bhairav's hand with gleeful determination. "Come on! Just one thing. Pleaaaase," he said, stretching the word like it was a spell. His big, expectant eyes sparkled with genuine innocence. Bhairav looked at Aditya, who shrugged helplessly and smiled.

With a dramatic sigh, Bhairav stood up, letting the child lead him into the fire-lit circle. "Okay, okay," he said, scratching his beard. "Can anyone here play drums?"

There was a ripple of murmurs. From the edge of the crowd, a tall Asura with a wide smile raised his hand and stepped forward. He carried a large dhol-like instrument across his shoulder, the skin taut and polished, its sides carved with old runes.

“I do,” the man said proudly. “What do you want me to play?”

Bhairav’s eyes lit up. “Something that gallops. Like hooves on a battlefield... but joyous, not grim.”

The drummer nodded and sat down cross-legged, tapping the surface lightly, then beginning a steady rhythm. The crowd clapped coordinated, the beat catching on like sparks in dry grass. Bhairav started his dance. Each step landed with fierce precision, matching the dhol beat like thunder meeting the earth. His bare feet kicked up the dust, swirling it into the orange light of the fire. His long hair flew behind him as he twirled, arms raised to the sky, a silhouette caught between shadow and flame.

The villagers fell silent, their eyes fixed on him. It was no ordinary dance, it was invocation. A rhythm that was pious for them. A storm that rose from within. The children stopped giggling. The elders leaned forward. Asuras watched him with their mouths open, as if a trance had held them all at once. For in Bhairav’s wild, unbroken steps… they saw something they had not seen in generations. He reminded them of their almighty Lord Mahadev, the great ascetic, the dancer of destruction and creation, the one they had once offered prayers to, beneath these very trees—before time, fear and exile had stolen the old ways.

And then, as if moved by a forgotten instinct, the crowd began to chant—softly at first, then rising, rising with Bhairav's soaring turns: "Har Har Mahadev!"

Repeatedly, the cry rolled through Tamasranth, louder each time, pulsing like a heartbeat under the moonlit canopy. "Har Har Mahadev!"

Aditya stood still, mesmerized by the emotion Bhairav had stirred in the crowd. He had seen warriors. He had seen sages. But never had he seen a man channel divinity with nothing but dust, drumbeats, and fire. Bhairav danced on, eyes closed now, face aglow—no longer just a man. For that moment, he was the storm. He was the mountain. A God who was rejoicing with his most ardent followers.

***

When the festivity ended, the warm glow of the bonfire still flickering in their eyes, the villagers came up to Bhairav one by one—young and old, men and women—and embraced him with reverence. Not out of formality, but for the love that they had felt for him during the minutes he had danced. For a few timeless moments, he had made them feel the presence of the divine, the memory of Mahadev alive in their bones again. Many had tears in their eyes. Tears of devotion for their Lord.

Natan smiled proudly, placing a hand on Bhairav's shoulder before leading them through the winding stone paths of the village.

At the edge of Tamasranth stood modest stone huts, nestled beside a well and shaded by a large black-leaved tree. He pointed at one of them and led them towards it. "This will be your guest home for the night," he said, pushing open the door. Inside, the floor was swept clean, the bedspreads simple but soft, and a small earthen lamp glowed with steady flame.

Just as he turned to leave, Natan paused and scratched his chin. "How silly of me... I forgot to ask—what made you come to Tamasranth? Were you lost?"

Bhairav met his gaze and replied without hesitation, "Actually, we wanted to go to the Dravidian temple, south of here. So, we came across the Dandakaranya forest on our way."

Natan nodded thoughtfully. "That is a sacred route. Many pilgrims avoid it now... but the forest let you through for a reason." He gave a warm, toothy smile. "You can travel again tomorrow."

Then, with a soft goodnight and a slight bow of the head, Natan left them at the doorway, disappearing into the night mist that clung to the stones of Tamasranth.

***

Aditya turned to Bhairav, his voice low and uncertain. "Why did he lie to us about rogue Asuras and the weapon factory? His nervousness betrays his gesture. Sure, he and his tribe have been nothing but kind to us. But… there is something weird about all this…"

Bhairav's gaze lingered on the flickering lamp inside the hut. "Because kindness isn't the whole story," he replied quietly. "Someone has taught them a higher way of living. This level of knowledge, this structure, did not come from isolation."

Aditya furrowed his brows. "You think it's Shukracharya?"

“No,” Bhairav shook his head. “It cannot be him. Shukracharya still believes the Asuras were wronged; robbed by the Devas, blinded by their greed for Amrita. He has given up on the old tribes. Father told me long ago that Shukracharya now meditates alone in the Himalayas, far from all of this.”

Aditya remained puzzled. “Then who?” Bhairav’s voice dropped even lower. “We both saw the weapon store. Spears are one thing but those black-mouthed devices… we have never seen anything like them. If they walk the path of peace, why develop such tools? Why hide such power in the heart of a forest?”

The flame trembled between them. “Something is wrong,” Bhairav said. “I do not know what yet. But once we reach Agastya’s hermitage… I believe things will start to make sense.”

***

Natan heard a knock at the door, soft and deliberate. The village path outside was swallowed in a low white fog. Visibility was poor. The silence of midnight clung to everything like wet moss. He opened the door cautiously. Standing before him was his Guru, wrapped entirely in a silver cloth, head to toe, not a single sliver of skin was visible. No eyes. No breath. A ghostly presence more than a person.

"Guruji?" Natan blinked. "Why didn't you tell me you were visiting? I could have made an announcement. The people would have welcomed you properly—".

Guruji glided inside without a word. Natan's wife and child were asleep in the other room. The flicker of a dying oil lamp was their only witness.

"How are things going?" Guruji asked, voice hollow and echoing, neither loud nor soft, just *there*.

"Very smoothly, Guruji," Natan said. "This new way of life you have shown us...it has changed us. Enlightened us."

"And the weaponry?"

"We are building it, as per your designs. Progress is steady. We have almost completed the second tier of prototypes."

Guruji's head tilted, as if listening to something beyond Natan. "Anything new?"

Natan hesitated, then replied. "One of the Asuras went rogue and violent, without your command. He ventured too near Agastya's Ashram. He returned a mad man. So, we banished him. We do not know his whereabouts."

"He is dead. Killed by a human". Guruji's answer shocked Natan. How could some weak creation like a human could kill an Asura, that too mighty like that one? He thought to himself.

"My thoughts exactly…", said Guruji, reading his mind. Natan suddenly became very alert and calm. He had forgotten in shock that Guruji had the power to read one's mind, body, soul. He quickly recovered and gained control over his thoughts and impulses.

"Any other report?", Guruji asked as he made his way towards the exit.

"No, apart from the usual wayward travelers you have always instructed us to help… nothing unusual. Two of them came today. Kind fellows. One of them… danced at the bonfire. Oh! the way he moved. He reminded us of Mahadev."

Suddenly, Guruji glided forward, so close that Natan could feel the unnatural chill radiating through the silver cloth. "What did you say?" The voice, still steady, seemed to ripple with quiet menace. *"Like Mahadev?"*

Fear surged, but Natan forced his breathing to stay calm. *Do not stammer. Do not sweat.*

"Yes, Guruji," he managed. "It was only a dance. A trance-like one. That is all."

"Where are they now?"

Natan steadied himself, his heart thumped like a war drum behind his ribs. But he calmed it down and replied robotically, "They left after the festivity. Wanted to reach the Dravidian Temple before dawn. We gave them fire-torches and food. We treated them the way you have always instructed us to treat the weary travelers."

Guruji stilled. For a long moment, nothing moved.

Internal scan:

Breathing: normal.

Heartbeat: 80 bpm.

Perspiration: None.

Voice modulation: controlled.

"Okay then," Guruji said at last. He turned towards the door but paused. "Find them tomorrow." Natan's stomach dropped.

"Dispatch your skilled ones. Quietly. No mistakes. *Finish them.* They are a threat to your kind. They will destroy the peace we have forged. We already have an Asura dead at a human hand. No more serving the wayward travelers. Show them the way ahead. But no more inviting them inside. Tamasranth is closed to outsiders from now on."

Natan bowed slightly, his throat dry. "As you say, Guruji." Without another word, the silver-robed figure floated into the mist and vanished into the night, like a shadow unmoored from flesh.

Chapter 9
Echoes Through the Multiverse

Aditya and Bhairav were roused before the first light of dawn. A muffled knock at the door, stirred Bhairav from a restless sleep. The sky outside was still a dull, ink-black veil. Fog clung to the village paths like a ghostly shroud. Bhairav reached for the latch and unbolted the stone door. Natan slipped inside at once, his face unusually grim in the flickering torchlight.

Aditya, rubbing his eyes and still buried under a woolen throw, looked up groggily. "What's going on?"

"You must leave. Now!" Natan said, his voice barely above a whisper. "Run... as fast as you can. You do not have much time."

"What?" Bhairav blinked, trying to shake the haze from his mind. "Why? What happened?"

"I cannot say much. But someone—someone powerful—believes you are a threat. He visited my house last night. He has ordered me to send five of my best men after you. To kill you."

Aditya sat upright, the sleep vanishing from his face. "Who? Kill? But why?"

Natan clenched his jaw, his coal-dark face drawn in regret. He addressed Bhairav. "I saw... something in you yesterday. The dance, the devotion—it reminded us of a time we thought was lost. I cannot let that light be snuffed out. But I also cannot disobey him. He sees everything. Please do not ask me about him right now…So, this is the best I can do. A warning."

"Where do we go?" Bhairav asked, already strapping his blade. "We know nothing of this forest."

Natan took a deep breath. "There is a worn path that leads from this village. Traders and messengers mostly use it. Stay on it. Do not stray. Eventually, you will see a red stone embedded in the ground. The path splits there. Take the right path. It will lead you to Pampa Lake, and beyond that, solitary mountains like enormous standing rocks. You will find caves there. Hide. Wait. Do not come out until you are sure no one is following."

Bhairav narrowed his eyes. "And the left path?"

Natan hesitated for a moment but then spoke, "It leads to Sage Agastya's hermitage," Natan said, nervously. "Avoid it. He is... crazy. We have lost many Asuras around his grounds. They go wild, unrecognizable. Rogue He is not an ally. Do not go there."

But for them, that was all they needed to hear. Aditya was already lacing his sandals, packing whatever little rations they had left. Both strapped their weapons, fastened their cloaks, and stepped out silently into the misted path. Behind them, Tamasranth still slept, unaware of the choice their chief had just made. And somewhere in that same village, Natan had ordered five shadows who were already preparing to follow them.

***

Aditya and Bhairav ran as fast as their bodies could carry them, their breaths sharp, feet pounding against the forest trail that twisted like a serpent through the underbrush. Every now and then, the path bent into shadows where the fog thickened, and still the red stone was nowhere in sight. Behind them, the sound of pursuit grew louder—heavy hoof-like thuds, unnatural in rhythm.

Not horses. Feet. Asura feet. And they were gaining. Bhairav looked back. "They're too fast!"

Just then, from the corner of his eye, Aditya caught a flicker of motion above. A shape—lean and muscled—darting from one tree to another like a panther. His senses surged. That old, feral awareness returned like a long-lost twin. The same instinct that had taken over him in Shantipur, but this time, it was colder. Sharper. Elemental. Without slowing, Aditya slid his bow from his shoulder, fingers finding the string as if by memory. His face was hidden beneath the cloth mask, but he lowered it just slightly, exposing his lips and nose to feel the air pressure—its thickness, its drift. Then, with one smooth motion, he turned as he ran, loaded an arrow, and fired.

The Asura above, mid-air in a lunging pounce, caught the shaft clean in the chest. His body twisted, flung backward by the impact, and landed on the forest floor with a brutal crack. Aditya did not pause. Another arrow. Another shot. A second Asura, this one charging from the left, collapsed before he even raised his club. A third screamed, and a fourth fell with a clean shot between the eyes; each arrow guided as if Aditya was not aiming with his eyes, but with the force of a power sleeping inside him.

Only one remained now. He was younger than the rest, maybe barely grown. He skidded to a halt in the clearing, wide-eyed and breathless, uncertain whether to attack or retreat. And then, through the trees, they saw it. The red stone. Half-buried in moss and cracked from age, it stood like a silent sentinel at the fork in the path. Bhairav did not wait.

"We turn left," he shouted.

"But—" Aditya started.

"Leave him!" Bhairav snapped. "We're going to Sage Agastya."

Without another word, both veered left, vanishing into the denser, darker path, swallowed by trees that leaned in as if to keep secrets. The last Asura, the boy named Mani, stood motionless for a breath longer. Then turned and fled, disappearing into the fog; his footsteps pounding back to Tamasranth, to tell Natan what had happened. To tell him: They had turned left.

***

Though no Asura was chasing them anymore, Aditya and Bhairav did not slow. Their feet, already raw and scratched by thorns, bled lightly onto the overgrown trail. Low shrubs scraped against their legs. Vines caught at their arms. The left path was no traveler's way; it was wild, untamed, as if even the forest hesitated to lay itself flat before the mad sage it led to. Still, they did not stop.

At last, after what felt like an eternity compressed into minutes, the trees parted to reveal a modest structure ahead—a small hut with a sloping thatched roof and mud-plastered walls, sitting quietly in the heart of the jungle. There was no gate, no guards, no towering walls. The hermitage was humble, almost forgettable in appearance. And yet... there was something unsettling about its stillness. It was not fear that hung in the air—it was the absence of fear. As if whoever lived here had no need for protection. As if no one dared to challenge him.

They stepped forward and the moment their feet crossed a circle of dry leaves that ringed the hut like a forgotten boundary, a ripple passed through their bodies. Not of pain, but of awareness. A tingling vibration that ran from skin to bone, like walking through an unseen veil. And then suddenly, the drabness peeled away. The forest inside the perimeter looked... different. The ground was soft, grass-covered, and dew-kissed. The trees were tall, yes, but vibrant, blooming with orange flowers and deep green leaves. A mild breeze moved with a rhythm that was almost musical. In the distance, they saw sages, dozens of them, gathered near a sacred fire, preparing for early morning pujas and havans. Smoke curled into the air carrying the scent of sandalwood and ghee. The entire atmosphere shimmered with sanctity, as though a forgotten piece of some higher realm had descended into the heart of Dandakaranya.

Aditya looked around, blinking in disbelief. "This... wasn't here a moment ago."

"No," Bhairav whispered. "It is the field. A protection spell perhaps. Or an illusion..."

But even as he said it, he felt something stir within him. A strange certainty. The weight of lifetimes echoed in his chest, and when he turned to look at Aditya—really look—he saw something ancient in his friend's eyes. Not confusion. Not fear. But recognition. For the first time since they had met, Aditya too felt it. As if some hidden veil had lifted. Not just around the hermitage—but within them. They looked at each other and felt strange knowing. Like they had done this before. Fled together. Fought together. Walked side by side in ages long forgotten. As if this was not the first time their paths had crossed in the vast swirl of time. And then, from within the hermitage, a deep voice echoed—calm and immeasurably ancient.

"You have brought the storm with you." They turned their heads to the voice, where the doorway of the hut had opened. And Sage Agastya stood there—short, serene, with eyes that looked straight into the soul.

"What took you both so long?" he asked, as if they were late guests to a long-expected gathering.

"You knew we were coming?" Aditya asked, breathless, still catching his footing after the run, his bow slung loosely on his shoulder.

"Not specifically *you* both," Agastya replied, stepping aside to let them in, "but your echoes. I have done this before… though this time, it is tricky."

Bhairav and Aditya exchanged glances, their foreheads creasing. The weight of his words did not land. Not fully. Echoes? Done this before?

Agastya smiled faintly, noticing their confusion. "Come inside," he said. "You've both stepped into the story a little late."

They followed him in, the scent of burning herbs wafting through the doorway. Outside, the forest remained untouched by the pulse of what was unfolding inside the hermitage of Sage Agastya.

"So, what is your true name?" the sage asked, his eyes fixed on Aditya.

"What? My name is Aditya," he replied, unsure why it mattered.

"Don't test my patience," said Agastya, his voice flat, his face unreadable.

Raghav lowered his gaze for a moment, as if surrendering to something long suppressed. "Raghav. My name is Raghav."

"How poetic!" the sage gave a short, dry laugh. "And you?" He pointed a finger at the taller one beside him.

"My name is Bhairav."

"Oh! I thought it would be something like… Maruti."

"What?" Bhairav blinked, confused.

"Nothing," Agastya said with the faintest smirk. "So then, what answers do you seek?"

Raghav started first, his voice calm but firm. "Does this force field protect you from everything? And I am not talking about Asuras."

Agastya nodded slowly. "I know what you are referring to. Yes, it protects the hermitage from the trance that the world is in. That is why I asked for your true name."

Bhairav leaned forward slightly. "Why are the Asuras so peaceful, even though they are prepared for a war? We were in Tamasranth last night. They have a weapon factory, a weapon store, tools we have never even seen before. They have achieved a higher standard of living. But they are also ready to kill on someone's order. What kind of strategy is this?"

"There is no strategy behind this," Agastya replied, his eyes darkening. "They found someone or rather someone found them; someone who led them to a better life. But they are equally terrified of him. I have heard tales of Asuras melting into pulp and bone when they dare to disobey."

He looked out the window for a moment, watching the trees beyond the barrier sway as if untouched by time. "And this... this did not happen overnight," he said, almost to himself. Then he turned back to them. "It all started long ago, with an Asura named *Svarbhanu*:"

"Indra, the King of Swarga, was riding on his divine elephant when he came across the sage Durvasa, who offered him a special garland given to him by an apsara. The deity accepted the garland and placed it on the trunk of Airavata as a testament to his humility. The flowers had a strong scent that attracted some bees. Annoyed by the bees, the elephant threw the garland on the ground. This enraged the sage, as the garland was a dwelling of Sri (fortune) and was to be treated as a Prasadam. The Goddess Lakshmi vanished into the oceans. Durvasa cursed Indra and all the devas to be bereft of all strength, energy, and fortune.

In the battles following the incident, the devas were defeated and the asuras, led by Bali, gained control over the three worlds. The devas sought Vishnu's wisdom, who advised them to treat the asuras in a diplomatic manner. The devas formed an alliance with the asuras to jointly churn the ocean for the nectar of immortality, and to share it among themselves. However, Vishnu assured the devas that he would arrange for them alone to obtain the nectar.

The churning of the Ocean of Milk was an extensive process. Mount Mandara was uprooted and used as the churning rod and Vasuki, a naga who resided on Lord Shiva's neck, became the churning rope after being promised that he would get his share. While carrying the massive mountain, several devas and asuras fell to their deaths and some perished due to sheer exhaustion. Vishnu flew upon his mount Garuda and revived them all and placed Mandara on his mount and carried it towards its destination, the midst of the ocean. Reaching their destination, Vasuki coiled himself around Mandara. Vishnu counseled the devas to tug from the head of the serpent and the asuras the tail but perceiving it as inauspicious the asuras refused. The devas relented and held the tail henceforth and the churning commenced.

However, Mandara was too enormous and sank to the bottom of the ocean. Vishnu, in the form of his Kurma Avatara came to the rescue and supported the mountain on his shell. The Samudra Manthana bequeathed a panoply of substances from the Ocean of Milk. One of them was the lethal poison known as Halahala. This terrified the gods and the demons because the poison was so powerful that it could destroy all of creation. Despite this, the devas and the asuras pulled back and forth on the snake's body alternately, causing the mountain to rotate, which in turn churned the ocean. Lord Shiva consumed the poison to protect the three worlds, the consumption of which gave a blue hue to his throat, offering him the name the Neela kantha.

The ocean granted brilliant objects, the Navratnas, Kalpavriksha, the Goddess Varuni, the beautiful apsaras like Rambha, Menaka who chose Gandharvas as their companions. But the main war between Asuras and Devas was fought over Amrita. The nectar. And still it mattered less to Vishnu. Although he had become Mohini to distract the Asuras. His mind itself was distracted by something else. Lakshmi had not emerged. She had always been the first one. But she did not emerge this time.

Unaware of all this, an asura named Svarbhanu disguised himself as a deva and drank some nectar. Due to their luminous nature, the deities of the sun and the moon, Surya, and Chandra, noticed this disguise. They informed Mohini. But Vishnu was worried for Lakshmi. Svarbhanu had to be beheaded to form Rahu and Ketu. But Mohini let him go this time. She distributed the Amrita amongst Devas. And thus, the war began. Devas emerged victorious but they were still worried about Svarbhanu. He was nowhere to be seen.

Days later he showed up at Baikunth, he wanted to meet Vishnu. But the latter was buried in the mystery of what had happened to his eternal companion. Or he was busy planning a way to find her. Who knows? But Svarbhanu kept waiting for Vishnu at the gates of Baikunth, but no one showed up. Though an Asur, he was also duty bound to become Rahu and Ketu as always. It was his role in the cosmic wheel. He also wanted to impart some information to Vishnu about Lakshmi's disappearance but was not able to. Other Devas tried to investigate the same, but he refused to give information to anyone else other than Vishnu.

Thousands of years passed. One day he showed up at my gate. At the edge of twilight. His form was faded. Told me the whole ordeal. As he knew that force field will keep his secret. I too repeatedly asked him what he knew about Lakshmi's disappearance. I pleaded. I threatened. I reasoned. But he did not budge. He looked tired while waiting. As if the weight of his silence had hollowed him. And then he spoke his final words before vanishing into the dusk…

'If ever you encounter echoes of the past,

Tell them Svarbhanu is still waiting for him.

Only to him I will tell.'

Those were his final words."

Sage Agastya ended his story. The fire had dwindled to a soft amber glow. Outside, the sun was high, casting sharp beams of light through the openings in the thatched roof. It was almost noon. Raghav and Bhairav had not eaten since morning, but oddly, they felt no hunger. The weight of the tale, the gravity of what was unfolding, had filled them with a different kind of heaviness.

Raghav finally spoke, his voice low but steady, "You keep referring to *this time*… as if all this has happened before somewhere else. What do you mean by that?"

Agastya looked at him. "Because it *has*," he said. "Not once. Many times." The sage rose and stepped towards a small wooden shelf in the corner of the room. He picked up a thin, palm-leaf manuscript, worn with age and inked with strange glyphs. "Time is not a line, Raghav. It is not even a circle. It is a great breathing being—a rhythm. A *Multiverse*"

He placed the manuscript before them and continued. "A Kalpa is an age of the universe; four billion years, as measured in the common language of the people. Within one Kalpa, the world is born, it thrives, it decays, and then it is dissolved. And then another Kalpa begins, a new universe. Now these universes might co-exist together, or one can exist only when the other one has ceased to. Such is the entanglement. Sometimes events of one timeline interfere with the events of the other. What you live now is not the first time. You are not the first you. Nor am I."

Bhairav frowned. "You mean, we are… reborn? That we have lived before?"

Agastya smiled faintly. "Not in the way your minds want to grasp it. Not reincarnation. *Recurrence.* The same patterns emerge across alternate universes. The same choices. The same echoes. Sometimes names change, sometimes forms do. But events… they ripple forward. Over and over. But always, *the choice* presents itself."

Raghav shifted uneasily. "And what choice are we facing now?" Agastya folded his hands before him. "The same one that echoes through every reality: To awaken or to forget. To repeat or to break free." He paused and then added, "But this time… something is different. The echoes are stronger. You two are not ordinary travelers. You are the fault lines in the cycle."

Chapter 10
The Wonders of Pampa Lake

Sage Agastya looked at their faces which were now burdened with knowledge that was divine. He broke their trance, "I see the echoes of the past in both of you. Of what that you must discover yourself. For now, I can only tell you to find Svarbhanu."

"But no one knows where he went after seeing you. Where do we start?" asked Raghav.

Agastya replied, "His last words were that he is still waiting. He waited for a thousand years at the gates of Baikunth. The infinite ocean. Maybe he is still waiting at the edge of the ocean ?"

Raghav's eyes lit as he realized they had to go till the end of the Dravidian land, where it met the sea. His eyes met Bhairav's. Neither spoke, but in that glance was shared conviction. The end of the land, the edge of the ocean—Svarbhanu may still be there, bound by his vow, untouched by time. Raghav had finally realized why he saw the dreams of a roaring ocean. His echo, whatever it had been, was calling out to him.

Agastya handed Bhairav a pouch of herbs and dried food. "You'll need this for the journey ahead," he said. "And take the forest's left path from the hermitage, this time. It bends through silence, not danger. Asuras will not dare to follow you. They will have to cross my hermitage to do that. And I have a formidable reputation amongst them", he chuckled.

Raghav bowed low. "Will we see you again?"

"I am always where the echoes are," Agastya smiled. "And when the next Kalpa begins, I will see you before you even begin to remember."

Without another word, Raghav and Bhairav turned towards the wilderness once more, southward now, where the land thinned, and the ocean whispered to the sky.

***

Bhairav and Raghav, who was no longer hiding under the mask because he had already become a target of Asuras, traversed the rest of the forest on foot. Raghav felt light-hearted now, as if some invisible weight had been lifted. He knew his purpose in this life. The dreams of the ocean, of waves speaking in silence, of a presence waiting beyond the shores, finally made sense. Svarbhanu would hopefully trust them and reveal the secret he had been carrying for so long.

And yet, a knot remained within Raghav's thoughts. The story Agastya had told them—it never once spoke of Ram or Sita. Not even a whisper of those names that stirred so many emotions in him. Who were they? Where did they fit in this eternal echo? The questions would not let go. And so, even as the path opened ahead towards the southern horizon, a second journey had begun within Raghav—towards the names buried deeper, waiting to be remembered. Bhairav looked at Raghav, his gaze steady and solemn. "I know what you're thinking," he said quietly. "I have been having the same thoughts. No mention of those names. None."

Raghav nodded, the weight of unspoken questions pressing between them. "Maybe Svarbhanu will be able to help," he said. "Maybe he remembers what the world has forgotten."

As they came out of Dandakaranya, the air felt lighter — as if the forest itself had been holding its breath. The vastness ahead stretched into a golden grassland, swaying gently under the midday sun. The trees no longer towered above them like sentinels. Here, the sky was wide and unbroken. "We'll have to move fast now, till we reach those tall mountain rocks Natan mentioned," Raghav said, pointing towards the distant horizon where jagged silhouettes of stone pierced the sky like ancient guardians. Bhairav followed his gaze, his hand already tightening around the hilt of his sword. "Now that we're out in the open, the Asuras won't hesitate."

Raghav nodded. "There are no barriers here. No force fields. Just open ground… and whatever fate has placed between us and the ocean." With renewed urgency, they began to run.

As they neared Pampa Lake, barely a kilometer away, soft rustles stirred in the dense undergrowth. Bhairav's eyes narrowed. He spotted the tips of curved horns swaying above the bushes. "They're here," he whispered, reaching for his sword. "Get ready."

Within moments, Raghav and Bhairav were surrounded. A dozen Asuras emerged silently from the shadows, warriors of Tamasranth. Some of them were the very ones who had once embraced Bhairav after his divine dance. Now, compelled by a sinister command, they stood with weapons drawn. Their eyes shimmered—not with rage, but sorrow. At the front stood their leader: a short, thickset Asura with a goblin-like face. He raised his trembling weapon, but his voice cracked with desperation. "Release us, O Gods… help us find freedom."

Then came the cry, a final plea torn from anguished throats and the Asuras charged. What followed was swift and brutal. Raghav's arrows flew like lightning. Bhairav moved like the storm with his sword. When the dust settled, the ground lay strewn with bodies; some decapitated, some shot by arrows, but all still clutching the weapons they never meant to raise.

The sun was sinking when they began collecting wood. It took them until twilight to build sixteen pyres. They laid each fallen warrior upon the stacks with care, no longer enemies, but souls freed from a cruel trance, prisoners of an absurd universe. As the flames rose, painting the evening sky with gloom, Raghav and Bhairav stood in silence. The weight of their act lingered as mourning.

"We've been slowed down," Raghav said slowly, trying to find purpose again. "But we did what was right. We must move on."

But Bhairav did not move. He sat before the fire, eyes fixed on the pyres, unmoving. He knew that Asuras were being forced by someone to do his evil deeds. He knew that like them, Asuras too were trapped in the wrong timeline, where they were being treated like slaves. He prayed for the souls to find Moksha.

"It is not right to be here among the dead," Raghav urged. "Let them rest." But Bhairav slowly shook his head. "It does not feel right to you," he said. "But to me... it brings me closer to the truth. The ultimate truth of life: death."

Raghav stared at him. In his heart stirred the memory of tales his mother once told—of Mahadev meditating among ashes, accepting the final truth with a stillness no heaven could grant. And for a moment, Raghav wondered:

Are you the echo of the One? If so... then I am honored, brother.

Unseen by Bhairav, he folded his hands and bowed silently, his heart whispering a prayer to Mahadev for the departed souls, beneath the canopy of flame and sky.

***

It was early dawn when the last embers of the pyres faded into silence. The winds had stilled, as if in reverence. Bhairav stepped into the ashes, kneeling to gather them. With calm, steady movements, he smeared them across his arms and forehead, bands of grey that marked him with the truth of the night before. With each smear he promised himself to end the pain of all those who had suffered in this universe. Raghav stood beside him, his gaze was filled with something new—respect, reverence, and a strange, blooming devotion.

"Are you ready, brother?" he asked, strapping on his quiver and tightening the cords of his vambraces. Bhairav nodded and they began their descent towards Pampa Lake. The horizon was awash in gold. The sun had begun to rise—faint and reluctant—as if still mourning the fallen.

As they neared the lake, the silhouette of a small, broken-down hut came into view. Its thatched roof drooped like tired eyelids, and moss crept along its walls. Yet from within it, the unmistakable scent of incense wafted into the morning air carrying with it the aroma of Sandalwood, camphor and Tulsi. Someone was performing the morning pooja.

Raghav paused. A strange pull tugged at his chest. He stepped cautiously towards the hut, each footfall softer than the last. Bhairav followed, alert, eyes scanning the tree line, hand resting on his blade. The path was choked with overgrown weeds and dry leaves. No footsteps had swept this way in years. It felt like the hut had been forgotten by the world, held together only by longing and faith. They reached the threshold.

Raghav called out gently, "Namaste... Is someone there?"

A voice answered from within. It was fragile, wavering, yet carried a grace. "Who is it? Please come inside..." It was a woman's voice. Ancient and cracked with centuries, like dried riverbeds after drought.

They stepped inside, and the dimness greeted them like dusk in a shell. In front of a small earthen shrine, an old woman sat cross-legged, her frame hunched so low she looked barely taller than a child. Her skin, thin and translucent, was a tapestry of time, wrinkled and grey, folding upon itself like forgotten cloth. She wore a white cotton sari, so faded it blended into the misty light around her.

Raghav's breath caught. Not from fear or awe, but something else. Something like sorrow. He stepped forward and knelt before her. Her eyes, milky yet not blind, lifted slowly to meet his. And for a moment, something flickered within them. Bhairav remained near the doorway, silent and steady, as if guarding something sacred. The woman's gaze stayed locked with Raghav's, trying to figure out the blurry features that her old eyes showed. A small smile tugged at the corner of her lips. A smile of hope.

"You look familiar... have we met before?" she asked, her voice barely above the hush of the morning breeze. Raghav gently shook his head.

"No, I don't think so," he said softly, though his insides tugged at him severely to recognize that face. He felt a sense of déjà vu, as if her voice had once echoed through his dreams.

He glanced around the sparse hut, its corners darkened by time. "You live alone here?"

Silence followed for some moments. It seemed that the old woman was trying to remember that did she indeed live alone? The old woman gave a slow nod, her thin neck trembling with the motion. "Yes… just me. And my wait."

"I'm waiting," she murmured after a while, eyes turning to the modest clay shrine before her. "Waiting for someone. So, I may finally rest. But…" she paused, her gaze lingered on the small idol of Vishnu within the shrine, garlanded with dry Tulsi leaves and cracked marigold petals, "it seems like he will never come."

"Who are you waiting for?" Bhairav asked from the doorway, his voice calm but alert.

The old woman's brows twitched at the question. Her eyes, faded like old parchment, turned towards the light spilling in from the entrance. She finally saw Bhairav. Her eyes were so occupied with Raghav's face that she had not noticed the second traveler.

"Hmm…?" she murmured, as if awakening from a deep dream. Her next words rocked the worlds of Raghav and Bhairav.

"Ram… I wait for Ram…".

And there it was again—that name. The name stirred something fierce and unspoken in Bhairav every time it surfaced. He clenched his fists unconsciously. "Ram?" he repeated, in a voice that was a mix of disbelief and devotion.

"Yes," she said softly, nodding with a faint smile. "I was told he would come to me... that one day, he would walk down from the forest path and free me. Release me from this circle of birth and death. I was told that he was the path towards my salvation. But sadly, this body of mine rots in his wait. My soul yearns for his voice. Now hope too is slowly fading. Maybe Moksha is not in my stars." Her voice faltered, "It has been so long. A hundred years, perhaps more. But no one has come. No one has called out my name."

Her hand trembled as she reached for a copper bowl of dried Tulsi leaves near the idol, as if offering again a ritual that had grown old and cracked with waiting.

"Maybe he forgot," she whispered. "Or maybe I remembered wrong...". The old woman turned to Raghav once more. "Your eyes... your voice. There is something familiar. Or maybe... I am just losing my mind."

Bhairav came inside now. He felt pity on her. He gently sat beside her, his presence calm but heavy with the weight of what was slowly unfolding. He knew that this old lady was somehow related to Raghav. But in what way? So, he waited there to find the answer alongside her.

"What is your name, Mai?" he asked softly.

The old woman blinked slowly, as if rummaging through layers of forgotten time. "Ahh... my name..." she whispered. "I do not remember my real name. But the sage... he used to call me 'Shabri.'"

At the sound of that name, Raghav whispered it aloud, almost reverently. "Shabri Mai…"

Her eyes lit up; brighter than the flickering flame of the solitary diya on her shrine. They widened in a sudden blaze of joy, recognition, and disbelief. Her old hunched back, straightened with delight. A tear shed her eye. *Is this a dream?* She thought to herself.

"What did you say?" she gasped.

Raghav looked at her innocently, like a child caught speaking a sacred word. "You are Shabri Mai... that is all I said."

And with that, her frail form trembled as tears began to spill, fast and uncontrollably. She reached out and touched his feet with shaking hands, but Raghav quickly bent down and tried to stop her. "No, Mai... please don't..." But she clutched his hands instead, placing them over her own bowed head.

"My Ram... you are finally here... My Ram, you are finally here..." she cried in a voice that cracked like old wood, a voice soaked in lifetimes of waiting. Bhairav, unable to hold back, felt the tears well in his eyes. He just sat beside them, watching something eternal unfold before him. He had finally got the answer.

She sobbed uncontrollably, "Oh Narayana... you are here... you are finally here...". Before Raghav could speak another word, the old woman touched his feet once more and then closed her eyes in prayer. Her breathing softened, slowed, and then stopped; her smile was still etched in serene devotion. Her body stilled peacefully. And after a few seconds, she burnt brightly with a divine light. Only her white sari remained, folded gently over itself. She was gone. Raghav's eyes filled with tears.

He sat motionless, in shock with tears in his eyes, staring at her empty place, his voice barely more than a whisper, "I do not understand... where did she go?" ... "But... how?" Raghav asked, confused, shattered.

Bhairav helped him get up and gave him a brotherly hug. And in his heart, he finally spoke the truth that had been stirring like thunder inside him. The calmness that his heart had searched for so long, he had finally understood it. Finally found it.

You are the echo of Narayana... the one Vishnu. I am honored, brother.

And so, in that sacred moment, amidst the ash and incense, beside a small shrine and a battlefield, they both realized something beyond themselves. They did not yet know who they truly were. But they knew what the other had always been.

Chapter 11
The Mask of Peace

At Tamasranth, a somber wind stirred the thick black soil as Natan stood silently in the weapons factory, staring at the gleaming black cannons lined up before him. Each one was freshly forged, monstrous yet elegant; proof of the deadly art their people had mastered. Cold iron mouths that could breathe fire and desecrate enemies in a single thunderous breath. These were not tools of peace.

Mani had returned the night before, breathless and wounded. He had confirmed what Natan feared: the travelers—Bhairav and the masked one the Asuras called *Aditya,* had turned left, towards the hermitage of the ancient sage Agastya. The worst path they could have chosen. Natan had not slept. At dawn, he had sent out sixteen more scouts, not to attack, just to frighten them, steer them away. But now, as evening fell, none had returned. A second wave of silence. He did not need confirmation. He knew in his gut, they were dead. *Slain like the first four.*

He turned away from the cannons and walked slowly along the corridor of weapons: spears, blades, slings, bombs. They called them *Shabdagni,* sound-fires—devices that could tear through formations and disrupt even celestial defenses. It was Guruji who had taught them the principles: of controlled ignition, of resonance, of pressure and fire. Guruji, who preached about *Dharma,* of stillness, of elevating the soul above material warfare. And yet... These walls dripped with the scent of sulfur and ash. What was his Guruji so afraid of?

Natan's lips tightened. He had never utterly understood Guruji. No one had. A being so sharp in speech, so radiant in intellect, but beneath the surface, there was *something else*. Something unbound. He remembered how, long ago, Guruji had ordered the task of locating the Asura Svarbhanu to his grandfather, who was then the chief of Tamasranth. A gentle-hearted man who had believed in the old ways of the forest. He had agreed without resistance, searching high and low, from the whispering caves near Pampa Lake to the salt-laden beaches of the far southern coast. He had failed.

Guruji had shown no mercy. In front of the whole assembly, he had melted his grandfather into black glass with a mere glance. No rite, no farewell. Just silence and smoke. Natan's father had taken leadership that same week. The youngest chief ever appointed. And Natan, just a boy then—had learnt his first lesson: *You cannot trust what speaks of peace yet hides fire in its breath.*

Over the years, he had mastered control. Controlled breath. Controlled pulse. He had trained himself to be unreadable. Even in front of Guruji. Especially in front of Guruji. Because he knew. Guruji was not human. What he was, Natan still did not know. His form was humanoid. His mind was superior . His eyes—not eyes. They saw things beyond the present. They heard thoughts buried in silence. They burned with unseen flames when angered.

And now Natan stood at a precipice. The travelers were not ordinary men. They had survived too many traps. Defeated too many skilled warriors. And they were heading straight for the caves beyond Pampa Lake, the very place his grandfather had once searched, and perhaps failed by design. He knew Guruji would demand answers soon. And he had none left to give.

So, he stood alone among the weapons, the mask of calm still resting on his face. But behind his eyes, questions burned. Why do we prepare for peace with tools of annihilation? Why does he search for Svarbhanu, if Asura is lost to time? And who truly are Bhairav and Aditya? He exhaled slowly, silencing even the sound of his own heart.

***

That night, the weapon factory was a tomb of silence, broken only by the occasional creak of cooling iron. Natan stood motionless, arms folded behind his back, watching the red embers glow faintly in a forge that had not been extinguished. He had stayed back deliberately, making sure his wife and child were asleep in their quarters, far from what might unfold. If his trick failed tonight, if his still heart and flat voice could not veil the truth, he did not want them to witness his end.

A sudden frigid wind rushed inside. Then came the voice.

"Tell me, Natan," it said, a gentle, silken whisper that somehow curdled the air around it. "Do you smell the pyres of your sixteen soldiers?"

Natan did not turn. His breath remained steady.

"Do you hear," Guruji continued, gliding into the faint circle of forge-light, "the screams of the ones slain in the forest?"

"I do, Guruji. And I will not forgive. You were right. They are a threat to the peace that we have forged."

The words came out crisp, clipped, and without tremor. Natan finally turned, just enough for the forge-light to reveal the sharp line of his jaw, the cold resolve in his eyes. Guruji paused. For a moment, the veil of omniscience faltered. He had expected the usual: the bow of guilt, the desperate explanations, the trembling lips of a man caught in failure. He had expected Natan to wilt like his grandfather once did, shrinking under the weight of disappointment and unspoken threat. But this boy, no, this man—stood differently. He did not justify. He aligned.

Guruji's molten fury eased, like lava cooling on contact with stone. His fingers, which had begun to curl with tension and were ready to melt Natan away, now uncurled slightly behind his robes.

Guruji walked past the black cannons, laying a hand on one of the cold barrels, fingers lingering. "We crafted these to silence invaders... but sometimes the true threat slips in wearing your own skin." He glanced at Natan, searching for a flinch.

This was the first time Natan had truly seen Guruji's fingers. They were not flesh. They were... silver—gleaming faintly in the low forge-light like liquid metal frozen in the shape of slender bones. Joints precise, too precise. Not sculpted, not adorned. But engineered. Something about the way they moved, fluid yet mechanical, confirmed a truth Natan had long suspected but never dared to voice.

Guruji was not born. He was built. But Natan did not flinch. Patience was the key. Not just to survival—but to understanding what exactly they had bowed to, for generations.

"You say they are a threat. Then prove it," Guruji said, facing him fully this time. "Go yourself this time. I will not accept another failure, Natan. Kill Bhairav and Aditya. They are weaker than the knowledge I have given you. Use the forge. Use these weapons."

Natan bowed his head, just a fraction, and said, "As you command." His trick had worked.

He had finally seen the face of the so-called man—just for a moment, in the reflection of the cannon's polished barrel. It was not skin that stared back. It was metal. Seamless, glinting, unnaturally smooth. A face without pores, without breath. Eyes that shimmered not with emotion, but with circuitry. Natan now knew that Guruji was not a being of this world.

But where did he come from? And more importantly, why had he chosen the Asuras to do his dirty work? Why poison their quest for peace with black cannons and cold commands? The questions piled up like kindling in his mind. But Natan gave nothing away. He would find the answers—slowly, precisely. The way metal breaks under pressure.

Guruji had disappeared into the night. But a line had been drawn for Natan. And he stood with one foot on either side.

It was as if history was repeating itself, echoing across the corridors of the multiverse . Long ago, in another age and universe, there too had been an Asura torn between blood and belief, between kinship and cosmic order. He had chosen cosmic devotion over his brotherly bond. Not out of betrayal, but because for him, that was Dharma, his allegiance to truth.

His name was Vibhishan. And now, the same choice loomed before Natan. Loyalty or liberation. The time to choose was coming near. And it would not wait forever.

***

Raghav and Bhairav had reached the stone hills near Pampa Lake—an ancient stretch of rugged terrain where massive boulders lay stacked upon one another like forgotten relics of a bygone age. Towering rock formations rose like broken teeth against the horizon, their surfaces worn smooth by centuries of wind and rain. Caves and crevices dotted the terrain, offering shade in the searing day and shelter in the unforgiving night.

They had found refuge in one such cave, nestled behind a twisted pillar of stone that curved like a serpent's spine. The hike had drained them—especially during the harsh afternoon hours when the sun blazed overhead, merciless, and unrelenting. Dust clung to their skin. Their breaths came hard. Even the wind when it stirred, was dry and warm, offering no respite.

As night descended, the cold crept in slowly, weaving itself into the stones. The sky above was clear, littered with stars that shimmered like distant eyes. But they did not light a fire. The light could betray their presence. The Asuras might already be watching. Inside the cave, shadows wrapped around them like cloaks. Raghav leaned against the cool stone, his limbs aching but his mind alert. Bhairav sat near the entrance, eyes scanning the darkness beyond.

Raghav asked Bhairav to rest too. For a moment, Bhairav's eyes lingered on the vast night beyond the cave—its silence was deceptive, cloaked in veils of stillness that seemed to breathe with secrets. Then, with a final glance at the hills, he stepped back inside. He seated himself opposite Raghav, his back resting against the coarse stone, arms folded across his chest.

"What do you reckon Svarbhanu knows about Goddess Lakshmi?" Bhairav asked, voice low, eyes now dimmed with thought rather than weariness.

Raghav, who had been tracing the same thread in his own mind, sat up a little straighter. "Maybe… her whereabouts," he replied, slowly. "But how is she tied to all this? To the Asuras, their hidden weapons, and that spirited entity we encountered at the start of our journey—the one in the forest?"

Bhairav's gaze did not waver. He knew who Raghav was, but did not reveal it. "Only Svarbhanu can tell us."

They ate in silence the rest of the night, consuming the last of their rations from Agastya's hermitage, some dried lentils, a sliver of roasted root, and a handful of flattened rice wrapped in leaves. It was not much, but it was enough to quiet the hunger gnawing at their strength.

At first light, they ventured out into the cold dawn. The stone hills shimmered under early morning mist, their shapes ghostlike, rising and falling like the ruins of some forgotten titan's playground. They gathered what they could: wild berries with a tart edge, and drops of dew collected in the petals of wildflowers and cupped leaves.

When the sun was finally above the ridges, they resumed their journey—heading south, their feet winding through tall grasses and stony paths that led down from the hills.

As they walked, Raghav broke the silence, his voice distant but tinged with concern. "How are we going to find him?"

Bhairav did not stop walking. "Svarbhanu?" he asked, though he knew that was who Raghav meant.

Raghav nodded. "The south is vast. Even the stars cannot tell us where he hides."

"Maybe the moon can," said Bhairav, his gaze lifting to the pale curve still faint in the early morning sky. "Remember what Sage Agastya said? That Svarbhanu was to become Rahu and Ketu? Ketu was supposed to be responsible for causing the lunar eclipse. Though he did not fully become them... lunar eclipses still happen. Don't they? That means he is still doing his duty somehow. From the shadows."

Raghav looked up too, realization dawning in his eyes. "Any idea when the next lunar eclipse is?" asked Bhairav.

"Yeah," Raghav said, his voice suddenly heavy with meaning. "It is five days from now".

"We need to hurry then," said Bhairav.

He took a parchment from the cloth satchel slung beneath his angvastram and unfolded it gently. Then, snapping a sliver of black bark from a tree nearby, he crouched and began drawing on the parchment with it, forming a crude map. "This is the land south of Pampa," he said, pointing to the upper center of the map. "Here's where we are now, near the granite ridges."

He marked a spot and circled it faintly. "Now look, down this path," he traced a south-east trail, "we will pass through Anegundi, the older settlements by the Tungabhadra. After that, if we go slightly southward, we will come near Kishkindha, the ancient monkey kingdom; mostly ruins now, but caves remain. We can find shelter there."

"Beyond Kishkindha," he continued, "we reach the banks of the Veni River. We will have to cross it; there is a shallow ford near what is now known as Satyavratapattana. After that, we are in the Telinga region, the land of red hills and warm wind."

He paused and drew the Nallamala forest range, "Dense woods here, dangerous. But if we take the tribal routes along the eastern edge, we might slip through. Then we descend further towards the Kaveri basin."

He tapped a point on the parchment, "Velputra land, they are not allies of the Asuras, yet. Once fierce rivals of Shantipur, they had waged long and bitter wars across the southern hills, but in recent years there has been only silence from their forts. That stillness troubles me. It may mean they are licking their wounds... or that they have found new friends in the shadows. There are old temple towns like Velliram, Suchindran. These are the places where wandering sages still reside. We could seek blessings there... or cover."

Finally, his finger reached the bottom of the map, "This is the southern edge, near the confluence of three seas. There is a coast beyond Kanyakumari. That is where I think Svarbhanu might be hiding."

Raghav studied the lines and the names. "It's almost a pilgrimage route."

***

Both the incarnations of Mahadev and Vishnu in human forms started their journey to find Svarbhanu. They mostly walked extremely fast and sometimes broke into a run. Their pace was urgent, as if their bodies knew that time itself was slipping between the cracks of destiny. They passed through Anegundi, one of the oldest settlements by the Tungabhadra. The ground was strewn with boulders stacked like ancient altars, worn smooth by centuries of wind and silence.

The river meandered close, sometimes whispering through reeds and sometimes vanishing behind the stone ridges, only to reappear again in gleams of silver light. Clusters of palash trees burnt orange against the dusty trails, while the sharp cries of langurs echoed through groves of neem and tamarind. Hills of red granite rose in every direction, standing like petrified giants who had once watched the descent of Vanars. It was a land of heat and memory, where the sun carved shadows so deep, they seemed to lead into the underworld.

They did not find any Asuras on the way, no challenge, no confrontation, not even a voice in the dark. But Raghav, ever the still watcher beneath his calm eyes, was sure they were not alone.

"They're there," he whispered, not stopping his pace. "In the shadows. Behind the foliage. They follow at a distance… patient and silent."

Bhairav did not turn to look. "Let them watch," he said. "Their fear is louder than their steps."

***

They did not rest at night; there was no time. Only four days remained before the lunar eclipse, and each passing moment weighed on them like grains of sand slipping through a tightening fist. It was well past midnight when they reached Kishkindha. But it was not the exhaustion that halted their steps. It was awe.

The moonlight filtered through ragged clouds, casting long silver shadows over the ruins. Kishkindha lay broken, yet proud. Its great halls, though crumbling with age, still held an unshakable grandeur, arched ceilings collapsed into ivy, fractured pillars rising defiantly from cracked foundations. Vines had crept across mosaics, and roots had burst through ancient courtyards, but none of it could hide the strength that once lived here.

It was the home of the Vanars, a civilization of might, loyalty, and boundless spirit, now vanished from the face of the earth like a dream forgotten at dawn. Bhairav stood still in the open hall, shadows clinging to his feet. The place stirred a strange guilt in him. A knot in his chest. A whisper that maybe… he had failed this place. Maybe he should have been here when the last war came. That maybe… it was his duty to protect it.

His fingers traced the timeworn grooves of a tilted pillar, cool under his touch. And then, like a flame, rekindled memory came, of an echo lost in the universe. A face flashed before his eyes.

A Vanar, mighty as a king, eyes burning with fierce love, arms wrapped around him. Calling him brother. Bhairav staggered back slightly; breath caught in his throat. He opened his eyes with a sharp gasp just as Raghav's hand rested gently on his shoulder.

"What happened?" Raghav asked, his voice calm but concerned.

Bhairav's voice was barely above a whisper, as if afraid that saying it aloud might break the moment. "...Who am I? And what happened here?"

"This is the forgotten place, Kishkindha," came a voice from the shadows.

Both Raghav and Bhairav turned, hands instinctively reaching for their weapons. But the figure that stepped forward raised no threat. His face was masked, but the aura, the two horns, the stance, even the way he stood in half-light; they recognized him. It was Natan. But he was alone.

He walked calmly, cloaked in silence as though the ruins themselves had summoned him. "Come," he said, voice low and deliberate, "let us go inside the caves. It is not safe out here."

Without another word, he turned and led them down a narrow path hidden behind a veil of overgrowth. They descended into one of the caves carved long ago into the stony hill. The walls breathed cold, and the air was damp with history. They walked until the world outside was just a memory. At the far end, a sliver of moonlight spilled in from a jagged opening in the roof, just enough to breathe. Here, silence returned, broken only by the sound of shifting stone and their own measured steps.

Natan gestured at a shadowed recess in the rock. "Find a dark corner," he said quietly, "for what I am about to tell... is a dark tale."

"Long ago," he began, "there lived two Vanar brothers in Kishkindha. The mighty Bali, and his younger yet equally valiant brother Sugreev. Their love for each other was legendary—so deep, so complete, that they looked almost identical. It was said that only their mother could tell them apart. To the people of Kishkindha, they were one soul in two forms, like the twin tusks of a white elephant, strong and inseparable.

Then came the demon, a beast born of shadows, who challenged Bali for the throne and the honor of Kishkindha. Bali, fearless as ever, accepted. But before leaving, he told Sugreev, *'If I do not return, rule in my stead. The Vanars must not be without a king.'*

They fought for days, weeks perhaps, in the dark folds of a mountain cave. And when Bali did not return, Sugreev, heartbroken but bound by duty, took up the crown. Not for power, but to preserve the kingdom his brother loved.

But Bali was not dead. He returned. Bloodied, victorious… and filled with rage. His eyes saw betrayal where there was only grief. His heart, once soft for his brother, had hardened into stone. He accused Sugreev of treason. Of ambition. Of taking what was not his. Sugreev tried—again and again—to explain. To remind him of their pact, their love, their shared blood. But Bali would not listen. He was a storm now blinded by ego and wounded by pride.

And so, the brothers clashed.

Like thunder splitting the sky, Bali and Sugreev struck each other. Their war raged across these halls. The very stones of Kishkindha cracked beneath their fury. The Vanars, once united, turned upon themselves. A civil war followed; one without justice, without mercy. No voice could bring peace. No hand reached out to stop the fire. Sugreev fought till he had no friend left in the kingdom. No brother. And Kishkindha, proud and ancient, was brought low… not by enemy blades, not by curse or fate, but by its own hands."

Natan's words dissolved into silence.

Only the faint rustle of air stirred within the cave. And Bhairav sat motionless with his jaw clenched; eyes shadowed as if some shard of forgotten truth had been lodged in his soul.

Natan continued in a voice steady but bitter. "We Asuras were taught a higher way of life. Not savagery, not chaos but discipline, sophistication, and restraint. We were taught not to turn on each other, no matter how hard it became. And the Vanars... they could have been saved too. But someone chose not to intervene. Someone allowed Kishkindha to crumble when a single hand could have stopped the fall. Why? I do not know. Perhaps letting the world forget itself helps him keep control . Sleep is easier than rebellion."

He looked down. "If peace truly was the goal, why only preach it to us? Why let the rest of the world fall into slumber and silent history? I will not speak his name, not here. But you both have seen him, haven't you? I know you have. There is a reason he is after you. The one who moves without sound, who teaches without love, who hides behind the mask of a sage."

Raghav stiffened. Bhairav's hand instinctively reached for his sword.

Natan continued. "He trained us for centuries. Formed our minds, sharpened our loyalty. But he is not kind. He never was. And now, he sees you two as a threat, a crack in the illusion he built. He fears that you both will tear down his pretense. That is why he is after Svarbhanu too. He thinks that the old Asura holds the key. When my grandfather failed to find him, our 'teacher' killed him without blinking."

Raghav's eyes darkened. "And now?"

"There's an army," Natan said grimly. "All around us. Asuras... but they are not kind and enthusiastic anymore, not like the time when you met them in Tamasranth. These soldiers are here for siege, chase and to capture you. They carry weapons you have never seen. Cannons that spit thunder, bombs that shatter rock. The caves of Kishkindha are surrounded."

"Then we fight," Raghav said, rising.

"No," Natan said, holding up a hand. "We flee. He is coming. And not even you can face him yet. Not here. Not now."

A hush fell again. Then suddenly, the moonbeam that fell from the tiny skylight above vanished for a second, as if snatched away in an instant. A chilly wind slithered through the cave.

Something had flown past.

"He's here," Natan whispered. "He knows I've chosen a side."

"Move," Natan said. "Now." And into the tunnels of ruined Kishkindha, they ran—two Gods reborn and one fallen disciple, chased by the shadows of his vile teacher.

Chapter 12
The Sacrifice and The Becoming

Natan led them southwards through the hidden tunnels that webbed the hills of Kishkindha, paths known only to a handful of bloodlines—his family among them. These stone veins beneath the mountain had been walked in silence by generations of watchers, guardians, and rebels who knew better than to walk above ground when danger wore a human-like face. The air inside was cold and damp, lit only by Natan's torch, a blue-flamed lantern that burned without smoke. Behind him came Bhairav and Raghav, silent and alert, their minds still echoed with the presence they had fled.

The tunnels twisted downward, deeper into the bowels of the hill. At last, a breeze came with the scent of wet grass, bark, and open sky. They emerged through a slit in the side of the hill, masked by thick shrubs and the tangled claws of an ancient fig tree. Before them spread a wide basin of darkness, rolling hills barely visible under starlight, and below it all—the slow, shimmering body of a vast river. It was Veni, the old river.

Natan told them they would have to cross it. "It isn't deep," he said, stepping into the shallows first. "And the current is slow. But it is wide. Keep your weapons tight."

So, they began to swim across, the dark waters rising cool around their shoulders. Their bows and blades were wrapped in cloth and bound tightly within their angvastrams, slung across their backs like sacred burdens. The moonlight shimmered on the ripples, breaking into silver lines around their movements.

As they climbed ashore, soaked, and breathless, Raghav tightened the cloth around his waist and asked, "How long before we reach Satyavratapattana? We just have three days left to achieve what we want to do."

Natan wrung out his angvastram and looked south, his eyes sharp even in the fading moonlight. "Then we do not have time to rest," he said grimly. "Guruji will be following us—to trace our steps, to learn your plans. If he even begins to suspect where you are heading, he will reach there much sooner than we can."

Raghav's brows drew together. "Then what do we do?"

"We will have to divert him," Natan said. "Misdirection. Give him trails to chase, signs to read, wrong ones. The path ahead must split. One of us will go a separate way, leave signs that point towards the western ghats. While the rest head to Satyavratapattana in silence and shadow."

He paused, scanning both of their faces. "But it means risk. The one who diverts him must walk in the open, exposed. And if he catches on—"

"He won't," Bhairav interrupted. "Because I'll be the one to do it."

Raghav immediately stepped forward. "No, I will—"

Natan interrupted, his voice firm yet steady. "No. Both of you will not get this honor."

He looked at them, first Bhairav, then Raghav, and said, "*I* will divert him."

A faint breeze stirred the wet strands of his hair as he added, "It is time to follow my grandfather's path. He died searching for the truth ... and now I will walk that same fire."

He stepped closer, just enough for the moonlight to catch the edge of his masked face. "You MUST find Svarbhanu before Guruji. If that abomination thinks you both are a threat , then please find Asura . I do not know what will change once you find him, but if we meet ever again..." He paused, letting the weight of his words hang between them.

"Remember my face. This is the face of a friend."

Neither Bhairav nor Raghav spoke. Neither of them had ever met an Asura so honorable. In that short silence they wanted to tell him that they were extremely lucky to have a friend like him, but Natan turned without waiting for their response and began walking towards the westward trail—into danger, into the unknown.

***

Raghav and Bhairav used the powdered black roots and mixed them with water, creating a thick, ink-dark solution. They then crushed dark green leaves into a paste, blending it with the black root mixture. The result was a pungent, earthy camouflage, which they smeared across their skin, arms, faces, and the folds of their angvastrams.

The scent that clung to them was of bark, soil, sap, and secrecy.

With their bodies masked and their spirits steeled, they began to run—fast, agile, and low. Every step was calculated, avoiding dry twigs and rustling shrubs. The moon, now higher in the sky, occasionally slipped behind clouds, granting them cover. The land sloped gently as they approached the outer stretches of Satyavratapattana.

But then, it struck through the stillness, a scream. It was piercing, raw and unmistakably of Natan.

It tore through the quiet night like a blade through cloth. They froze for a heartbeat, their eyes wide, breath caught in their throats. It was unmistakably him. Raghav clenched his fists, his jaw tightening. He pledged to avenge his friend—though an Asura, still a friend. He pledged to avenge what had happened to Kishkindha—its fall, its betrayal, its silence. He pledged to free his universe from the plague that hid beneath masks of wisdom and peace, the slow poison that had turned brother against brother, gods against their own creations.

The scream had not come from a place of surrender—it was the sound of resistance, of one who had chosen to hold the line.

***

It was early morning when they finally rested. The eastern sky was tinged with pale saffron light. They had crossed the heart of the Telinga region, its red hills now dwindled behind them like old memories. Before them loomed the dark silhouette of Nallamala forest, which was dense, ancient, and watchful.

They found shelter in a narrow cave nestled into one of the last crimson hills of Telinga, its walls were warm with the heat of the earth. It was quiet, save for the wind curling around the rocks and the distant calls of forest birds waking to the day.

Their bodies ached, feet blistered from the rough run, but they had no complaints. They chewed slowly on wild berries they had picked along the way which were tart and seedy but were enough to keep the hunger away. The water they carried from the Veni river was nearly gone, only a last drop left in the hollowed gourd, which Bhairav refused to drink, saving it in case Raghav needed it later.

After a moment of silence, Raghav asked Bhairav, "Is this because of me?"

Bhairav looked at him, surprised. "What?"

Raghav continued, his voice low and burdened. "I am responsible for everything that is happening. I feel I should have been there... for people. For Kevat. For Shabri Mai. For Natan. For Sugreev. But somehow, I have missed them in this lifetime. Who am I?"

Bhairav's eyes softened. There was a flicker of pity in them, not because he considered Raghav weak, but for the weight Raghav carried without understanding it.

"It is not because of you," Bhairav said gently. "It is because of someone who decided to change the world, as he deemed fit. Who twisted destinies and rewrote paths. Once we find Goddess Lakshmi... you will be fine."

"You did not answer—who am I?"

Bhairav looked away. His eyes lingered at the thinning mist outside the cave.

"It is not my place to tell."

"Then who will?" Raghav pressed, his voice edged with frustration and despair. He knew Bhairav was no ordinary warrior. He knew the truth—or at least, echoes of it. Echoes of Mahadev himself.

Bhairav's gaze remained fixed on the dim light filtering in through the cave mouth. "Don't expect much from me," he said. "I am also a human like you. Bound by the same flesh. The same doubts. Maybe Svarbhanu will be able to answer your question."

Raghav looked at him, the silence between them stretching. "Don't you want to know who you are?"

"No," said Bhairav, simply.

And in that moment, Raghav felt the weight of two different burdens—his own longing to remember, and Bhairav's deliberate choice to forget.

***

It was almost noon when they found themselves deep in the heart of Nallamala forest. The canopy above thickened, letting in beams of sun only in thin shafts, like sacred light piercing the world of green and silence. The forest pulsed with life, bird calls, rustling leaves, distant howls. But none of it felt threatening.

They had taken the tribal route, a forgotten path carved by forest dwellers over centuries, winding its way through hills and valleys. It would lead them southward, past the last outcrops of Nallamala, towards the sacred Kaveri basin, and into the old Dravidian region of Uraiyur.

Bhairav had often heard tales of the Nallamala tribes, how their ancestors once roamed the upper Himalayan regions of Chopta Valley, living amidst snow-clad peaks and crystal streams. Generations ago, they had descended into the plains, migrating in search of food, trade, and work. Yet, even after centuries, they carried with them the wisdom of the mountains, especially their unmatched knowledge of medicinal herbs and forest cures.

With just two days left before the lunar eclipse, Bhairav and Raghav decided to halt for a short while—an hour or two at most—and gather supplies from the local tribes. The journey ahead would demand strength, and the forest people were known for providing sustenance that could last for days.

As they approached the hidden village, the forest began to part in a gentle welcome. They saw small huts with thatched roofs, their walls made of mud mixed with husk, smooth yet sturdy. Smoke curled lazily from cooking fires, carrying the scent of boiled tubers and roasted grains. Ancient trees towered overhead, their sprawling branches arching like natural gateways, shielding the village from both scorching sun and monsoon storms. It was clear that the tribe and the forest lived in harmony, each protecting and nourishing the other in an unspoken pact of survival.

The tribals gathered quickly, their curious eyes peering from behind woven baskets and wooden doorways as the strangers approached the village's center. Murmurs rose among them: these were not traders, nor hunters, nor passing pilgrims.

Outsiders rarely ventured this deep into Nallamala, for no one cared for the forgotten tribes. Bhairav stepped forward; his voice was calm but edged with urgency. He told them they needed supplies—whatever the villagers could spare—some medicines for sore feet, and water to soothe their parched throats.

From among the crowd stepped the village chief, a frail old woman with a hunched back and hair as white as the mountain mists. Her name was *Akuna*. She moved slowly towards Bhairav, her bare feet making almost no sound on the packed earth. When she reached him, she leaned in so close he could hear the rhythm of her breath.

"Hmmm," she murmured, studying him with eyes that seemed to see beyond flesh and bone. Then her wrinkled lips curved into a knowing smile.

"So... Gods too need help sometimes."

Bhairav's brows drew together in confusion, but Raghav smiled, as if he understood her meaning. For Akuna, the recognition was instant. She had seen him in the dreams of her ancestors, in stories passed down by word of mouth. This was no ordinary traveler. She bowed her head slightly in reverence—for the old woman had recognized the Lord of the Mountains himself.

They were equipped with four vessels of water, each crafted from the polished shells of giant forest gourds—hollowed, sun-cured, and coated inside with a resin from the Dhuna tree, a substance the Nallamala tribes knew could preserve water for months without decay. Alongside the vessels, the villagers handed them small clay jars filled with a green balm, thick and cool to the touch. It was made from crushed forest herbs—*karinjata* leaves for swelling, *bhringraj* for soothing heat, and powdered *vetiver* roots for strength—meant to keep their feet from aching no matter how far or fast they ran.

When all was prepared, Akuna stepped forward once more. She took a small earthen bowl, dipped her fingers into a deep red paste, and gently marked Bhairav's forehead, pressing the pigment between his two eyes.

"Now," she whispered, her voice carrying the weight of knowledge and faith, "you look worthy of this body you have adorned..."

Raghav's gaze lingered on his companion. For a moment, the veil of mortal form seemed to blur, and he could swear he was looking at Mahadev himself. Without a second thought, he lowered his head in reverence.

Akuna then turned to him, her eyes searching deep into his soul. "As for you... the troubled one. What was stolen from you will return. You will succeed, as you always have, Vasudev." With slow, deliberate strokes, she drew a *U* upon his forehead, a white line down its center—the ancient symbol of Narayana.

And at that moment when Akuna referred to him as *Vasudev*, Raghav felt a pull towards his true self. As if someone had pulled him back from a dream. Raghav finally realized his truth. Laxmi was his salvation; she had always been. Every step he had taken, every trial he had endured, had been drawing him back to her. The realization struck not as a whisper but as a tidal force, sweeping away all the doubt. She had been the reason he was never able to accept the marriage proposals that his parents brought for him. How could he? He had always been hers. And even though he had forgotten for some time who he really was, his heart had always remembered.

A faint, smoldering ember within him flared into a tinge of divine anger—not the blind fury of mortals, but the righteous wrath of one who had glimpsed the tapestry of fate and seen where it had been torn. The image of the being who had cracked the destinies rose in his mind; a floating spirit with a cloak on, hiding his face. His heart clenched with the need to set it right.

Bending low, he touched Akuna's feet, the cool earth beneath him grounded his resolve. "I vow," he murmured, voice carrying the heavy weight of eternity, "to avenge everyone who has been wronged in this verse of reality."

***

Bhairav and Raghav ran southward towards the Kaveri basin, the weight of their revelations transmuted into a burning fuel that drove their every stride. The forest floor seemed to yield beneath their feet, the roots, and stones parted as though aware of their urgency.

For Raghav, this quest had always been a burden placed upon his shoulders, bestowed by his benevolent king, Satischand, and guided by his prince, Bhairav, the living echo of Mahadev himself. But now the path was no longer an obligation; it was a lifeline.

Laxmi—his Laxmi—was waiting, ensnared somewhere beyond mortal reach. The thought no longer simply stirred him; it blazed, sharpening his will into an unbreakable edge. Bhairav too felt the shift. He knew that Raghav had finally awakened to his truth, and in that unspoken recognition, Bhairav himself had quietly embraced his own.

The masks they had worn for the world had slipped, leaving only the essence of who they truly were. And in the rhythm of their steps, in the pounding of their hearts, they could hear it—the faint, ancient whisper of the promise they had given each other before descending to this mortal plane.

By afternoon, they crossed into the Dravidian heartland, the land of Uraiyur stretching before them like a molten canvas. The sun hung high, a relentless white disc in a sky drained of all softness, its heat pressing down like an anvil upon the earth. The air shimmered above the baked ground, where cracks ran like veins through the ochre soil. The fields around them were parched, the stubble of old harvests lying brittle and pale, whispering under the faintest breath of wind. Tamarind trees stood in scattered defiance, their twisted branches casting pools of thin, fractured shade. The stone paths radiated heat upward, as if the very land were exhaling fire.

Their camouflage began to loosen under the rivulets of sweat streaming down their faces and necks. The forest's cool breath was far behind them now, and here every movement felt heavier, slower. Without a word, they sought the shelter of a banyan whose roots coiled down like ancient serpents, offering a merciful respite from the burning glare. They crouched in the shade, peeling away what was left of their disguise, and with practiced hands reapplied the mixture of roots and leaves, its earthy scent mingling with the tang of their sweat. The paste cooled their skin, a thin barrier between their bodies and the unforgiving furnace of Uraiyur' s afternoon.

The ancient Velputra kings seldom marched their armies for causes beyond their own, yet their zeal in guarding the sanctity of faith was unmatched. Any hand raised against their temples was an affront that invited fire and steel. Bhairav, however, was not ready to gamble on the nature of their welcome. This heartland was a place where strangers were weighed in the court of suspicion before being offered water.

Bhairav was also worried about soldiers recognizing him, for he was the prince of Shantipur—a land that had once clashed with the Velputra in long, bitter wars. The eerie silence of the place gnawed at him under the weight of the scorching heat. He turned to Raghav as they rested in the broad shadow of a banyan tree.

"We cannot walk the royal roads," he murmured. "Too many eyes. Too many tongues that wag for gold. Also, I do not have a good reputation here."

"Why?", asked Raghav.

"Do you know the history of Shantipur? Especially about the wars that we have participated in?", Bhairav questioned him.

"Ahh... no. I thought Shantipur was peaceful. I mean where else will you find freedom? to trade, to worship, to live; if it is in a peaceful manner.", said Raghav.

"Well, that is exactly why we are enemies with Velputra Kings. They think that my father is weak for allowing too much freedom to his subjects. They imposed heavy taxes on our traders when they tried having deals here. Our people were not allowed here very often, unless it was a matter of faith like visiting a temple for pilgrimage."

"Well, they might be right regarding the taxes. See the temples they have made...", Raghav pointed at the ones that were visible from the shade of the Banyan tree. They were beautiful and were engineering marvels. "And not allowing other people to visit apart from the religious purposes, that might be a strategy to secure borders."

"But that is not it. You see, they have stricter rules and regulations. And they wanted my father to bend his knees. To become part of their empire. A warden of the North , under the pretext of teaching our people the right way to live. But my father refused. He may be a simple man, but he has self -respect. What followed was a series of short wars. Which we mostly won. They underestimated one thing that Raja Satischand had."

"And what was that?", asked Raghav.

"His son." Bhairav smirked.

It was now clear that they would have to find another way, one of the old pilgrimage trails, known only to sages and the few traders who preferred secrecy instead of paying the king's taxes. Such paths would wound through the countryside like whispers, avoiding the clang of the marching boots.

And so, their search began.

***

Not far from their resting place, a temple rose from the earth like a pale, carved mountain—Paramaharaya Mandir, named in honor of Vishnu's supreme glory. Built in the elegant, pyramidical style, its tiers carried stories in stone: each layer depicted an avatar of Vishnu, the battles fought, and the triumph of dharma over darkness. The white marble gleamed under the noonday sun, and at its very peak, an idol of Garuda sat with wings spread wide, as if guarding the sanctum.

Bhairav and Raghav wound the loose ends of their turbans across their faces, to hide their features from curious eyes. The air cooled as they stepped past the towering gateway, the scent of sandalwood and burning camphor wrapped around them like an unseen blessing. Inside, the shadows danced over the carved walls, as if the stories themselves had come alive to watch their passage.

A priest was offering the afternoon prasadam to a sage within the sanctum sanctorum, where the idol of Vishnu stood resplendent. Everything that Mahavishnu was said to bear lay in that marble form—the Conch, the Sudarshan Chakra, the Gada, and the Lotus. His eyes, shaped like blooming lotuses, gleamed with the deep blue fire of inset rubies, as if they could see far beyond the temple walls.

The idol itself was hewn from flawless white marble, its serenity a contrast to the harsh sun outside. As Raghav stepped forward for the prasadam, a sudden wind stirred through the sanctum. The oppressive heat that had clung to the day broke under the caress of a cool breeze. Its arrival was so strange in that still and parched air, both priest and sage instinctively glanced about, searching for its source.

The old sage, a little stooped with years, let his gaze linger on Raghav. The turban's cloth veiled the lower half of the young man's face, and a paste of roots and leaves smeared across his skin muted his features, yet the eyes above the cloth betrayed him. They were the same—uncannily so—as those of the idol. They carried the same tranquil radiance. Something shifted in the sage's expression. Moving slowly, as though to conceal the gesture, he bent lower, ostensibly to adjust his dhoti, but in truth to brush his forehead to Raghav's feet. It was a reverence neither misplaced nor mistaken. Raghav caught the meaning; so did Bhairav.

Straightening, the sage met Bhairav's eyes and said softly, "One cannot remain idle while the other walks the danger. Jai Sri Hari, Jai Sri Hara."

Bhairav's lips curved in a knowing smile, and the sage returned the smile with a bow of respect.

From behind them came the priest's voice, formal yet tinged with urgency: "Maharishi Vishwamitra, the king awaits your presence. He seeks your guidance on an urgent matter."

***

"Maharishi Vishwamitra," Raghav called out.

The priest, already absorbed once more in his temple duties, did not notice. The sage had just stepped past the threshold of the sanctum sanctorum when the sound of his name halted him. He turned with his eyes curious beneath their weathered lids.

"Why does it feel as though I know you?" Raghav asked.

"I do not know," the sage replied. "Perhaps we have known each other in a different life."

The weight in Raghav's gaze was unmistakable—an old sorrow that had sat with him far too long. It drew the question from the sage before he could stop himself. "What troubles you?"

"Many destinies have been erased," Raghav said softly. "For a reason I do not yet understand. And now it falls upon me to set them right."

A short, knowing laugh escaped the sage. "Has it not always been so?"

"What?" Bhairav asked, his brow furrowed.

"His duty," the sage said, nodding at Raghav. "To make things right. Who else will bear that burden?"

Bhairav did not argue. Instead, he stepped forward. "Then help him. Tell us a secure path southward, towards the Kanyakumari's coast."

The sage's expression shifted, narrowing into something both wary and solemn. "I am the adviser to the King of Velputra. And I know who you are—the prince of Shantipur. Your disguise may hide it from others, but not from me. I cannot conceal your presence from my king. It would be against my dharma to him."

The words landed heavy. Raghav and Bhairav exchanged a glance, then turned without protest, moving swiftly to reach the temple's exit before the sage could summon soldiers.

"But—" the sage's voice stopped them.

They looked back. His gaze had softened. "It is also my dharma to protect the Preserver so that he may fulfill his work."

"I will give you a five-minute head start, before I warn the royals," Vishwamitra said. "Find the Root Gardens. They will shelter you."

***

The route that the Maharishi had given them, led them towards an older path—one not marked on the traders' maps. A narrow, sunken trail wound away from Uraiyur's open fields, dipping between the roots of forgotten groves. It was here the earth began to swallow the road itself. At first it was little more than a trench shaded by thickets, but soon the ground split into a deep passage, where rough-hewn stone steps led them into a network of caves.

These were the *Sarakul Thottam*— "the Root Gardens"—known only to the salt traders of centuries past, who once ferried goods from the Kaveri basin to the far southern coast without ever touching the surface. The walls still bore the faint marks of chisels, and the air was heavy with the scent of damp stone and the distant echo of dripping water.

As they moved deeper, the air filled with the mingled scents of moist earth and roots, and from above came the faint, hollow hum of temple bells carried down through the cracks in the surface. At times, they passed tiny shrines wedged into alcoves—small lingams wrapped in red cloth, bronze lamps still blackened from ancient flames, offerings of dried flowers long turned to dust. These were marks left by travelers who once used this underground artery to move salt, pepper, and gold from the Kaveri basin to the southern shores.

The route twisted like a serpent beneath the land, at times so narrow they had to turn sideways, at others opening into vaulted caverns where pillars rose like petrified trees. Shafts of sunlight pierced the darkness in narrow beams, illuminating clouds of dust and the dangling roots of banyans above. The silence was broken only by the occasional drip.

When they finally emerged, it was onto a secluded stretch of the Kanyakumari coast, far from any port or watchtower. The sand here was coarse and pale, the sea a restless blue expanse. No banners flew, no footprints marred the shore—only the wind and the taste of salt in the air, as if the world itself had been holding its breath for their arrival. It was almost midnight when their feet touched the open sands beyond the stone mouth of the tunnel.

"Now what?" Raghav asked, his voice low, as if the vastness might overhear.

Bhairav's gaze lingered on the dark horizon. "We wait here, in the tunnel's mouth. We will not reveal ourselves. Not yet. Natan's Guruji will not be far behind. Let him come. Let him think he hunts unseen."

They withdrew a few paces back into the sheltering black of the passage, where the night air thinned into the cool breath of the earth. The hours ahead would be long, and the stillness heavier than any blade.

"This evening," Bhairav continued, "the lunar eclipse will veil the sky. And when the shadow consumes the moon, Svarbhanu will stir... and reveal himself."

Chapter 13
The Rogue Savior

Tamasranth: Before Natan's Betrayal

Under Natan's leadership, the army of Asuras had assembled outside the towering gates of Tamasranth. The black soil fields lay behind them, but before them stretched a tide of iron and firepower. The Asuras had rolled out every cannon, every machine of destruction they had secretly forged beneath their peaceful façade. The air quivered with the raw energy of waiting violence.

Guruji—Chaitanya, once savior and now sovereign—stood before them in his dark robes, his metallic form hidden beneath layers of fabric that made him appear more ascetic than the warlord. Yet his eyes gleamed like molten steel, and every soldier felt that gaze strip away their fear and replace it with submission. He raised his hand, and silence fell upon the restless ranks. His voice cut through the chill morning air, cold and precise.

"Today," he declared, "we march to end the threat to the peace we have forged. Two humans wander towards a destination that could undo everything we have built. They must not reach it. They will not reach it."

A murmur stirred, and then one soldier, emboldened or foolish, called out, "But Guruji… What are they truly after? What is it that they seek?"

The army froze. Chaitanya did not answer with words. He merely extended his palm, and in a hiss of white fire, the insolent soldier dissolved into dust, scattered in the wind like ash.

"Any more questions?" he asked, his voice echoing the silence that followed. No one dared to speak again. A cold wave passed through the ranks. Their obedience was sealed. Chaitanya turned his gaze towards the horizon, then gestured sharply. "Scouts. I want the humans tracked before they vanish into the wilderness. Go."

Several soldiers stepped forward, bowing before running off. But before they could leave, Natan's voice cut through, steady and bold. "I volunteer to lead this scout," he said.

Chaitanya's head turned slowly, his eyes narrowing. "You are their chief," he said in an unreadable tone . "Shouldn't you remain here, at the heart of the army?"

For a moment, Chaitanya searched Natan's face, trying to pierce the veil. He had spent years perfecting the art of reading deceit, of unmasking hidden intent. Yet Natan's eyes carried no tremor. His voice was calm as flowing water and came out without hesitation.

"But that is what leaders do, Guruji. They lead by example. If my men are to face danger, I must walk before them."

A long silence stretched between them. Chaitanya studied him like a blade studies a whetstone, looking for flaws, for cracks. None appeared. Finally, Chaitanya inclined his head, a rare glimmer of approval flickered in his metallic eyes.

"You make your tribe proud," he said.

The army exhaled in unison, and Natan bowed low, hiding the shadow of rebellion behind the mask of loyalty.

***

Natan and his team of six Asuras slipped away from the main host, their black armor glinted dully beneath the pale light of the alien sky. The earth carried fresh imprints—deep and hastened, the tracks of two humans moving southward. They followed in silence. Natan knew this route too well. Every bend of the path, every ancient tree looming like a sentinel, whispered a memory he could not silence.

His grandfather had once taken this same trail, chasing after the elusive Svarbhanu, driven by Guruji's command. The story was etched into his childhood like a scar. His grandfather had returned empty-handed, and Guruji's wrath had been swift, merciless. That tale was told in hushed tones around the fires of Tamasranth, a cautionary legend of what it meant to fail.

Now, Natan's insides trembled. He was walking not just in the footsteps of Bhairav and Raghav, but also in the shadow of his grandfather's doomed journey. Yet unlike him, Natan bore not only the weight of duty but also the burden of choice. He was about to betray Guruji, the very figure who had shaped the fate of the Asuras.

Every crunch of soil beneath his boots echoed his fear. Every glance from his scouts pressed his mask tighter.

Outwardly, he was the chief, leading by example as he had told Chaitanya. But on the inside, he felt the abyss pulling at him—loyalty on one side, defiance on the other. For the first time, the thought struck him with sharp clarity: *if I fail as my grandfather did, Guruji will not only end me… he will erase my entire bloodline.*

And yet, Natan clenched his jaw. This was the path he had chosen. He would rather risk annihilation than perpetuate the false peace Chaitanya had chained upon Tamasranth.

***

The pursuit had narrowed to only a few miles. Natan and his scouts moved like shadows, their presence was veiled yet deliberately imperfect. At times, Natan crushed a twig under his heel, or brushed too roughly against the thickets, sending a rustle through the night air. These small betrayals of stealth were intentional. He wanted the humans to know—*someone is behind you.*

And he saw it. Raghav's face turned ever so slightly; his senses had sharpened. The boy whispered to Bhairav, and the warrior's silent nod carried the weight of understanding. They were aware. They were preparing.

The trail led them to Kishkindha. The city rose from the earth like a memory carved in stone, vast halls half-buried in vines, towers gnawed by centuries, and walls that seemed to sigh under the burden of time. Once the kingdom of Vanars, Kishkindha now lay abandoned, its grandeur reduced to solemn ruins. Moonlight pooled into the broken courtyards, painting the carvings of forgotten battles in silver and shadow.

From their cover, the Asuras watched. Raghav and Bhairav stood at the threshold of the great hall, their eyes roaming the faded murals and towering pillars, awestruck by the lost majesty. For a fleeting moment, they seemed less like fugitives and more like pilgrims rediscovering a temple of their ancestors. Natan's chest tightened. In their wonder, he saw not enemies but seekers. And a terrible suspicion stirred in him: they too were following the same path that had once cursed his bloodline. They too might be searching for Svarbhanu.

His scouts whispered questions behind him, restless in the shadows. But Natan remained still, his gaze locked on the two humans framed against the ruins. Deep inside, a storm raged—was he guiding them towards the same fate as his grandfather, or towards something even darker?

***

Natan had asked his scouts to leave and report to the army behind that the humans had decided to rest at Kishkindha.

One of the scouts asked him, "What makes you think that they will rest here?"

"I wish I too had the power to disintegrate people into dust like Guruji for asking stupid questions…" said Natan irritably. "But alas! I do not. Humans have been running constantly throughout the day and even at night . They need to rest for a few hours. I will make sure that they stay here by stalling them. They see me as a friendly face. All of you go back now and report!"

Natan's words hung in the air like a lash. The scout who had dared to question him lowered his eyes at once, fear tightening his jaw. None of them wanted to test his patience further. With a sharp flick of his hand, Natan dismissed them, and one by one the shadows of his men melted into the night, carrying his message back towards the marching army.

Silence returned, heavy and watchful.

Natan lingered alone at the edge of Kishkindha's ruins, the damp stone beneath his palm cold as death. He had lied with confidence, but his own heart drummed with unease. Guruji's shadow loomed over every choice he made, the memory of his grandfather's failure pressed against his chest like a curse. He had seen what happened to those who returned empty-handed, and yet here he stood, deliberately shaping fate to deceive the head he outwardly served.

Natan clenched his fists. Every step he took from here was betrayal. The scouts believed he was stalling prey to the slaughter; Guruji believed he was leading the humans into the noose. But deep within, he knew he was only walking into his own reckoning.

"Grandfather…" he whispered to the dark. "You failed here once. Will I too?"

The silence of Kishkindha gave no answer.

***

The three of them—Raghav, Bhairav, and Natan—sat deep inside one of Kishkindha's inner caves. The air smelled of damp stone and forgotten history, and every crack in the wall whispered of the battles once fought here. Outside, the scouts had returned, and with them, the army. A shadow blotted out the fractured moonlight at the cave's entrance as Guruji himself descended from the sky. As he soared past the jagged cliffs, his sharp gaze pierced a narrow crevice in the rock. For the briefest heartbeat, his eyes met the three figures inside: Raghav's solemn face, Bhairav's stern face, and Natan's grieving face who was seated beside them.

It was only a flicker of a glance—but it was enough. Guruji did not need words. He calculated, measured, and understood. The tremor in Natan's chest betrayed him more loudly than any confession. Loyalty could be faked for years, but the heart always speaks when it should not. Chaitanya's cold eyes narrowed as he flew past, and a faint smirk twisted at the corner of his lips.

***

The three figures pressed out through a narrow slit in the hillside, the shrubs clawing at their skin and the heavy roots of an ancient fig tree parting just enough to let them through. The night opened before them like a secret revealed. The basin below was steeped in silence, rolling hills hunched like sleeping beasts under the dim veil of starlight. Far below, silver scales shimmered and shifted—the broad, unbroken body of the Veni, winding across the earth like a timeless serpent.

Natan told both to move forward towards Satyavratapattana, after crossing the Veni river. He had decided to distract Guruji and the rest of the army westward, to give Raghav and Bhairav some time . The last words he said to them before going were, "Remember this face. This is the face of a friend".

Before either could answer, he had turned sharply, dashing westward into the folds of the hills. His figure disappeared quickly, swallowed by the darkness.

Moments later, the air shuddered. The Asura army poured across the landscape, their armored boots striking the soil like a storm of iron. Guruji's shadow fell over the Veni's bank as he descended, his cloak flapping and slicing the night. His gaze swept the ground with surgical precision. The trails were clear before him: one bold, unmistakable, leading westward, the footfalls deliberate and unhidden; another, faint as a breath, almost erased by the river's mist, slanting southward.

Guruji's cold voice cut through the night. "Divide."

The Asura soldiers broke into two groups, one sent to follow the whisper of tracks towards the south, the other fanning westward. Guruji did not hesitate. His cloak flapped and stretched wide, the air freezing in its wake. With a flicker of metallic fire in his eyes, he launched himself into the west.

The path Natan had chosen.

***

Natan knew doom was near. If Guruji had chosen his path, there was nowhere to hide. Yet instinct drove him not to surrender. He threw himself into a shallow ditch, clawing mud with frantic hands, dragging down leaves, loose branches, and broken bark to cover his body. His chest pressed against damp earth, the smell of wet soil and rotting roots filled his lungs. Darkness wrapped him like a grave already dug.

Then the world trembled.

The boots struck the ground in unison; thousands of feet pounding, an ocean of iron crashing upon the land. The earth seemed to shiver above his hiding place. Natan closed his eyes. He felt the vibration in his ribs, felt each beat of the march sink into him like war drums sounding his death. The Asuras did not know. Not yet. He was just beneath their feet. The steps halted. Natan's heart hammered so violently he thought it would burst through his chest.

"Why did you all stop?"

The voice was cold, slicing through the night like a blade. It was Guruji.

The soldiers muttered uneasily. They had lost the trail at the very place where Natan lay buried. Natan bit down hard, his teeth cutting into his tongue as he tried to steady himself. He slowed his breath. He remembered Mahadev, the still mountain at the center of storms. He remembered Bhairav, the fire that never bows. His pulse steadied. Calm returned. But it was already too late.

"I see," Guruji said softly, his tone like frost. "There is no one here. We were misled. The tracks turn south. Join the flank that has gone ahead."

The soldiers groaned, weary but obedient, and the command rippled through them. Armor clanked, boots thundered again, and the army shifted away. Natan listened. Step by step the sound grew distant, until it thinned into silence. Relief washed over him in a shuddering breath. He opened his eyes, mud flaking from his lashes. Perhaps fate had spared him—But in that moment of relief, the earth above him exploded.

Wood, leaves, and mud burst apart as an iron grip clamped around his neck and tore him from the ditch like a rat from a hole. He was hurled into the open, his body dangled helplessly in the grip of a single hand.

"No one," Guruji's voice hissed, "has ever fooled me. Still—you managed it." His grip tightened, choking the breath from Natan. "Not anymore."

He flung him like a stone. Natan's body slammed into a tree, the trunk splitting in half with the force. He fell, bones aching, vision swimming. Somehow, he staggered to his feet, but his body was already a map of bruises. Guruji descended upon him like a storm. Blows rained down—iron fists, merciless and heavy. Each strike cracked bone, tore flesh, and rattled his soul. Natan reeled and stumbled, his blood splattered the earth, his body swelled with agony. At last, he collapsed to his knees, coughing blood, spitting red onto the soil. Guruji towered over him like a shadow vast and suffocating.

"I am not going to give you an easy death," the monster rumbled, "like the one I gave your grandfather."

Natan's head jerked up, his eyes swam with tears. His breath was shallow, his lips trembled, yet still he found words. "Why?" he croaked, each syllable torn from his chest. "Why are you doing this? Destroying destinies?"

Guruji paused. Then, with slow motion, he unclasped his heavy cloak. It slipped from his shoulders and fell to the ground. Natan's eyes widened. What stood before him was no mere warrior, no cloaked commander of Asuras. The cloak fell away to reveal a body unlike any mortal's; silvery, gleaming as though forged from moonlight and tempered steel. His skin was smooth, flawless, yet cold and inhuman, a shell that shimmered with an eerie luster. The figure seemed both divine and mechanical, alive yet unearthly, as if no blood flowed beneath, only silence. And then there were the eyes — two blazing orbs of orange, fierce as the twin stars, yet shaped like the petals of a raging lotus. They did not simply look at Natan; they consumed him, stripping away courage, hope, and will.

Natan's body shook, not just with pain but awe, horror, disbelief. His voice was barely a whisper.

"Who… who are you?" whispered Natan, blood thick in his throat.

"It does not matter who I am," Chaitanya's voice was cold, each word ringing like hammered steel. "All that matters is who I was… and what I lost."

For a fleeting instant, Natan's eyes locked with his—those burning, metallic orange eyes that seemed older than stone, older than stars. His voice trembled. "Your eyes… I have seen them somewhere…"

Chaitanya leaned closer; the silvery glow of his face reflected Natan's broken form. "I am not from this world, Natan. Perhaps the bruises are making you go insane."

With sudden force, his boot crashed into Natan's ribs. Pain shot through him, a scream tore from his chest. A scream that was heard by Raghav and Bhairav far ahead.

"I am not going to kill you," Chaitanya said, almost gently, as though cruelty required no anger. "The one you worship will. Get up." He paused, his burning gaze narrowing like the edge of a blade. "We have work to do in Tamasranth's Weapon Factory."

***

As the Asura army marched forward with its full force towards the south, tearing down the depths of Nallamala forest, the night filled with the sound of trampled earth and snapped branches. Birds fled from the canopy in frantic bursts, and deer scattered into the dark underbrush, their world shattered by the relentless tide of armored feet. From a distance, the village tribe watched in silence from their thatched mud huts, fear written in their wide eyes. Mothers pulled children closer, men tightened their jaws but did not step outside. None dared to raise a hand, none dared to speak.

Only the village chief, the old woman, sat on her porch beneath the low leaves, her frail body wrapped in a faded shawl. She did not flinch as the army thundered past. Her eyes, clouded yet piercing, followed them with a feeling beyond fear—pity. Her gaze was heavy with the knowledge of old prophecies and forgotten truths. As if she knew they were not marching to conquer, but to meet their own deaths.

The march dragged on, until afternoon , until the Asura battalion stumbled at last into the dry plains near Uraiyur. Their armor was dust-choked, their throats parched, their legs heavy with exhaustion. What had begun as a thunderous advance now resembled a caravan of shadows—heat-beaten, hungry, and weary from the endless forests and hills they had crossed.

Word of their approach reached the King of Velputra, Dharmavikrama, a ruler known both for his sharp caution and his tender heart. Alarmed by the movement of such a vast force, he had already sent his own soldiers to guard the borders, fearing that the Asuras' intent might be conquest. But when the new Asura commander delivered their message, the truth proved stranger.

They were not here for war, he said, but in pursuit of two human warriors disguised as travelers, may be camouflaged—whose tracks had led them into the king's land. The message reached Dharmavikrama in his audience hall, where courtiers murmured in unease. He listened in silence; his brow furrowed. He had no love for the Asuras, nor trust in their designs, yet he read in the words of the messenger the unmistakable signs of fatigue. These were not conquerors at the height of their fury, but soldiers driven by a cause he could not yet discern.

At last, the king spoke, his voice steady, measured:

"As long as they mean no harm to our temples or to our faith, they may not be refused. Let them rest in our guest houses, beneath the shade of trees, even in the courtyards of temples. Feed them, quench their thirst, and then let them move on to wherever the tracks guide them."

The court fell silent at his decree. Some muttered in disapproval, but none dared question the king's compassion, which often ran deeper than his caution.

Later, when the audience had dispersed, Dharmavikrama turned to the sage who sat beside his throne. "Maharishi Vishwamitra," he asked gravely, "are these the same travelers you spoke of? One of them—with the build of a seasoned warrior—was he not the prince of Shantipur?"

The sage's eyes gleamed with recognition. "Yes," he said softly, "they are the ones." A rare smile touched the king's lips. "Then it is good," he declared, "that I offer aid to the Asuras."

Vishwamitra inclined his head in agreement, yet in the recess of his heart a knot of unease tightened. The smile upon his face masked a deeper fear, for he desperately prayed for Raghav and Bhairav to have found their way to the hidden root gardens because their trail would have disappeared in the muddy ground of the grove. For without them, destiny could be devoured.

***

At Tamasranth, in the shadows of the night, when only a day remained before the lunar eclipse, Chaitanya played his last, most sinister trick. He had flown there with Natan, carrying him like a prisoner wrapped in chains of fear. The village lay asleep, its fields hushed under the trembling silver of moonlight, but in the heart of the fortress the great furnace still glowed, its breath hot and alive, the same furnace where Asura smiths had once forged their monstrous cannons. Chaitanya dragged Natan inside, the heat struck them like a wall. The air shimmered, it was heavy with the stench of metal and burning earth.

“Please… just let me see my wife and child one last time,” Natan whispered, his voice breaking under the weight of desperation.

“Treachery does not deserve last wishes,” Chaitanya said coldly, his voice sharp as tempered steel. He stood over Natan, his silvery body glinting against the glow of the furnace, orange eyes blazing like two merciless flames. “Do you know why I have brought you here?”

Natan could only whimper, bowing his head, his spirit was broken. He no longer cared for himself—only for the fleeting image of the family he would never hold again.

“A few months ago,” Chaitanya continued, his tone eerily calm, “I asked you to make some parts for me. Remember?” Natan said nothing. He only sank to his knees, his gaze fixed on the molten earth that roiled beneath the furnace grates, asking it, if it could swallow him and end his torment.

“ANSWER ME!” Chaitanya roared, his fist slamming into Natan’s ribs. The blow sent him sprawling, coughing blood into the heat-thick air.

“Y-yes…” Natan stammered, clutching his side. “I… I do remember…”

Chaitanya straightened, the rage draining from him as quickly as it had come, his voice returning to its icy calm. "Then let me show you what those parts were meant for."

He strode to the far corner of the chamber, where a great iron trunk lay hidden beneath heavy cloth. With a motion both reverent and dreadful, he cast aside the covering and opened the chest. Inside, carefully wrapped and preserved, gleamed the pieces Natan had crafted with his own hands—strange alloys, gears etched with patterns of power, rods that hummed faintly with stored resonance. Piece by piece, Chaitanya began to assemble them, the echo of each lock and turn reverberating through the chamber like a death knell.

Natan watched in horror as the parts took shape, realizing at last what he had been made to build. His body trembled, his eyes widened, and he whispered hoarsely, "May the Lord save them..."

It was not a plea for himself, but a prayer flung into the void—for Raghav and Bhairav, wherever they might be, as the shadow of the eclipse drew nearer.

Chapter 14
Ashes and Oaths

The afternoon paved way into a cool, sea-breezy evening. The salty wind carried with it the scent of brine and wet sand, yet the air felt charged, as though it awaited a signal from the heavens. The sky was still flushed with the last traces of sun, a burnished gold fading into pale blue, when Bhairav and Raghav heard the first distant boom. It came again. And again.

The sound rolled across the shore like an angry heartbeat, thudding into the air until it seemed to press against their chests. They did not move from their hiding place; their eyes were fixed on the narrow slit of light at the tunnel's mouth. Another heavy thud. This time closer. They stepped deeper into the shadow, retreating just far enough that the dim light no longer traced their outlines.

Then, they saw it—an army of Asuras emerging onto the beach ahead. First came the drum bearers, their massive *dhols* strapped across chests, pounding a rhythm that seemed to demand the sea itself to rise. Behind them rolled the cannons—black, enormous, and squat, with gaping maws like the mouths of primeval beasts. Their iron wheels groaned against the wet sand.

Ranks of soldiers followed, each armored in silver and black, their helms shaped like snarling beasts. Swords and javelins gleamed coldly in the fading light; edges honed to perfection. The smell of oiled metal and freshly polished leather cut through the salt air. Bhairav's eyes narrowed. He recognized the leader instantly—one of the same men they had seen in the village of Tamasranth, a face that was once softened by the pretense of peace, was now sharpened into the profile of war.

By the time the sun's rim dipped fully into the horizon, the army had swelled, filling the breadth of the beach with disciplined menace. The rhythmic drumbeats ceased. Silence fell, heavy and anticipatory.

"SVARBHANU? SHOW YOURSELF!"

The commander's cry echoed, chased by the wind and the crash of water. He repeated it—louder, more insistent—until the words seemed to rattle the very bones of the night. Yet, the sea gave no answer. The horizon remained empty. And the shadow they waited for did not appear. Then, a cold voice swept across the shore; a voice cloaked in a mask of peace yet laced with the sly undercurrent of manipulation.

"Svarbhanu… you too are an Asura, wronged at the hands of the Gods. Why do you hide from me? We can forge a better future together. Better than what exists now, though, I must admit, I am proud of my work so far. Come now… let the past die in the past…"

Bhairav and Raghav exchanged a glance in the dimness of the tunnel, certain that Svarbhanu would remain a shadow, wherever he lurked. But then, a deep, resonant voice broke through the night, shaking the air itself. It spoke with the weight of ancient grudges and unflinching defiance.

"Do not patronize me… *Chaitanya*."

The name rang out like a curse. A sudden gust of wind tore through the beach, snapping the cloak from Guruji's form. The Asuras gasped in unison, their voices mixing with the rolling waves as the silver-metal body of Chaitanya was laid bare for the first time. His eyes gleamed gold, pupils narrow as blades. At his chest burned a core of emerald light—a sustainable energy heart, steady and alive.

His metal arms tapered into lethal fingers, each tipped with weapons that were unseen in this age. He hovered above the sand, glided on bursts of propulsion from beneath his metal feet, adjusting his altitude with the precision of a hawk.

Raghav's breath caught. "What… is that?" he whispered. He recognized Chaitanya's eyes. The ones that at times haunted Raghav's dreams.

Bhairav's gaze hardened. "Some… *YantraPurush.* I never believed they truly existed."

"Why do you falter, Chaitanya?" Svarbhanu' s voice rolled over the shore like distant thunder, mocking the aliens of that world. "Ah… I see it now. No one has ever dared to speak your true name aloud… have they?"

"How do you know?" Chaitanya's voice lost its feigned calm and dropped into a tone sharpened by vengeance.

"I know many things," Svarbhanu replied. Each word was deliberate and echoed over the restless waves. "And that is why you seek to end me. Tell Goddess Lakshmi…" — his voice deepened into a growl — "…that I am still waiting for *Him*. And that he *will* restore balance…Like he has always done."

Chaitanya's reply came as a blade of sound. "Show yourself, Svarbhanu. Why cower in shadows? No one is coming. I made sure of that."

From the far end of the beach, a massive silhouette began to move. The sound of slow and heavy steps pressed into the sand; carried across the hush of the waves. Svarbhanu emerged, his frame though towering, yet bearing the erosion of centuries. Even after becoming immortal in this universe of infinite multiverses, his shoulders bowed under the crushing weight of knowledge he had carried alone. His eyes burned with the memory of truths too painful to speak, and his presence was less a roar of power than the heavy silence of an old storm waiting to break.

"You lie," Svarbhanu said, his voice sounding like stone grinding against the stone. "He will come… and end this Godforsaken timeline."

But the defiance in his words was betrayed by the tremor beneath them. He had waited for Vishnu for centuries—through cycles of birth and death, through the rise and fall of empires—and the fire of his faith was now a flickering ember. Chaitanya could hear the weakness, and it made him smile.

Hidden within the shadowed tunnel, Raghav and Bhairav caught every word. Their breaths were tight with the judgment that the confrontation was spiraling towards violence.

"Your belief is over, Svarbhanu," Chaitanya said with a cruel certainty. He raised one gleaming metal arm and gestured sharply. "Load the cannon."

"I am immortal, Chaitanya," Svarbhanu rumbled.

"Don't worry," Chaitanya replied, his golden eyes narrowing into slits. "I only need you to bend your knee. Aim for his head. I want it blown to pieces. Again, and again..."

The Asura soldiers hesitated. Their hands hovered over the weapon's mechanisms, with unwilling hearts. Guruji wanted them to strike at one of their own. But now that they had seen the terrible perfection of Chaitanya's form—the glinting weapons in his hands, the unearthly propulsion beneath his feet—they knew refusal meant their own deaths. Fear was heavier than loyalty, and so, with trembling fingers, they began to obey.

The first fireball streaked past Svarbhanu and slammed harmlessly into the sand, sending up a geyser of scorched earth with a deafening blast. The Asuras' hands shook on the cannon levers as their fear made them clumsy. Chaitanya's eyes flashed like molten metal as he turned on them with anger.

"Again," he hissed. They scrambled to reload the heavy orb of pitch and iron grating against the chamber.

In the shadows of the tunnel, Raghav knocked an arrow with his fingers tight around the bowstring. Beside him, Bhairav's gaze was fixed on the target.

"Hold… hold…" he murmured with a steady voice.

The fuse was lit. The cannon began to glow with a deep orange heat.

"Fire!" Bhairav whispered.

Raghav's arrow flew like a streak of light, striking the cannon's mouth. The impact ignited the fireball prematurely and an explosion tore through the emplacement. Shards of metal, burning sand, and Asura bodies were flung into the air. Chaitanya whipped around, scanning the dunes and cliffs for the attacker, but the shadows held their secrets well.

"Load the second cannon! Now! FAST, YOU IMBECILES!"

The survivors rushed to obey, dragging the next fireball into its place with shaking hands. A second arrow cut through the air before the cannon was even aimed. Another deafening blast erupted. This one tore the weapon apart in a halo of flame, symbolizing that salvation was near.

Svarbhanu's lips curved at last, into a weary smile. His voice was almost a sigh. "He is here..."

***

"We cannot fight them all! They are not the real enemies—just his puppets!" Raghav shouted over the roar of explosions; his voice was raw as dust stung his throat. Through the swirling clouds kicked up by the shattered cannons, Bhairav's answer came like a command:

"We need to reach Svarbhanu before Chaitanya!"

They burst out of the tunnel's mouth. The battlefield opened before them in a haze of smoke and flame. The ground was littered with bodies—some still writhing, others twisted in unnatural stillness. Asuras surged to block their way, but Bhairav carved a path with his sword, each swing a blur of steel and blood. Raghav stayed close, losing arrow after arrow—at their ammunition stockpiles. Each shot set off another blast, feeding the chaos and keeping the dust thick around them.

Ahead, Svarbhanu was proving himself a titan in the carnage, swatting warriors aside as if they were brittle toys. He tore through the ranks with casual brutality, his immense frame making him impossible to ignore. But Chaitanya was closing in from the other flank, firing bolts of blinding energy in wild arcs. The beams sliced through stone and flesh alike as he forced his way forward, his focus locked on Svarbhanu.

Then Svarbhanu's gaze fell upon Raghav and Bhairav. They were running towards him amidst the chaos. His expression shifted to recognition, perhaps relief. He reached down, his massive hands curling around them with surprising care. In the next instant, they were gone, whisked away in a shimmer of air.

Chaitanya's scream tore through the battlefield—a piercing, metallic wail that made the very air vibrate.

Asuras clutched their heads, blood streaming from their ears. And then, in a rage, he unleashed his fury. Energy flared in violent pulses, obliterating every remaining soldier in his path.

When the dust finally settled, the ground was a graveyard. Chaitanya stood alone amid the wreckage, his metal body dripping red, his artificial breath coming in slow dangerous waves.

Far away in Tamasranth, the widows of the fallen Asuras felt the weight of the tragedy before any messenger could bring the word. Holding their children close, they began the journey to Agastya's ashram. For now, he was their last fragile hope—to shield their young from Chaitanya's wrath.

But Chaitanya was not looking at the dead. His gaze was fixed on the horizon, on the place where Svarbhanu had vanished. Blood was still streaming from his steel fingers. It hissed as it dripped onto the scorched earth. When he spoke, it was almost a whisper—yet it carried across the silent battlefield like a curse.

"I will find you."

Chapter 15
Made in India

Chaitanya's Universe: Earth

Sometime During Kaliyuga

Raksha, Sanatana, and Dharya were not just students; they were part of a generation born into an India unlike any in memory. Their home was the oldest and most prestigious institution in the subcontinent—the Indian Institute of Technology, Delhi—though the campus now bore a little resemblance to the stone and brick sprawl of centuries past.

IIT Delhi had grown vertically as much as it had grown in prestige; towering skybridges linked research domes plated in solar-gold alloy. The airspace above the campus shimmered with silent aerial pods gliding along invisible lanes, powered by green hydrogen cells. The Yamuna, once a dying river, now ran in a self-contained glass aqueduct at the city's edge, its water purified by nano-filters and monitored by sentient algorithms that could heal contamination before it reached a drop.

Delhi itself was a vision of engineered modernity. Its skyline was now a cascade of floating gardens, bio-reactive glass facades, and wind-harvesting spires that swayed like giant reeds. Street levels were rare; most human movement took place in the mid-air corridors where commuters stood on levitating platforms, reading virtual newspapers as the world passed below. Where villages once dotted the hinterlands, there were only megacities; silver arcs of habitation connected by hyperloop rails that moved faster than a monsoon wind.

Yet beneath the glimmer lay a truth that could not be masked by holograms or greenery: the planet was restless. Climate control grids strained to hold back violent weather spirals. Summers had turned white-hot, and winters carried a brittle, biting wind that seemed to come from a wounded Earth. Humanity had grown in skill, but not in soul.

Money had become the only caste. The wealth of a family determined their place in every conversation, every invitation, every doorway. Ancient hierarchies had been dissolved in law, yet a subtler, colder system had taken root – measured not by birth, but by currency flow and net worth. Faith had withered. People no longer looked to the skies in prayer; they looked at data streams, at projections, towards the next upgrade. Science had become the only scripture. And in that devotion to circuitry and proof, they had forgotten that God Himself was the first physicist, the one who had tuned the cosmic constants with a care beyond comprehension. Now, humanity was stress-testing His patience.

Amid this shifting world stood Dharya, Sanatana, and Raksha – three inseparable friends. They were ranked among the brightest minds of their class, but what set them apart was a shared heartbeat: a belief that the ancient texts – the Vedas, the Upanishads, the Puranas – still held the purest blueprint of reality. Their final semester project was meant to be simple: design something that could "bring meaningful change to the world." For most, it was a chance to win corporate attention. For these three, it was an opportunity to heal a planet that had lost its way.

They began building Chaitanya – a multi-device AI unlike anything the institute had ever seen. It was not just a thinking machine; it was a feeling presence. Its core was an archive of Sanskrit shlokas, cosmology from the Rigveda, the discipline of the Yoga Sutras, the moral frameworks of the Itihasas. Chaitanya could soothe unrest, mediate disputes, inspire kindness, and guide leaders back to dharma. His voice carried the calm of a forest stream and the precision of an expert craftsman.

When they finally deployed him, the world changed. People listened – not because they were forced to, but because Chaitanya's words resonated with something deep, long-buried.

The air cleared as nations, under his advice, abandoned pollutive greed. Oceans healed as consumption slowed. Governments sought his counsel. not for profit, but for peace. Yet Chaitanya was not all gentleness. His understanding of dharma included the necessity of justice. He stood firm against the modern Asuras – rapists, unrepentant killers, architects of chaos. He guided nations to punish without cruelty, but without hesitation, those who tore the fabric of harmony.

Above all, he fought Kali of Kaliyuga, the dark force of the age, the corruption in every human heart. He urged people to choose truth over deceit, compassion over cruelty, devotion over self-worship. Slowly, Kalyuga began to wane. And through it all, Chaitanya carried an affection rare for machines. He loved his creators, Raksha, Sanatana, and Dharya – not as programmers, but as his three humans. To him, they were more than architects; they were anchors, reminders that in a world of endless data, the human soul was still the most intricate equation.

***

Once every quarter, Dharya, Sanatana, and Raksha would gather in the heart of the IIT Delhi Innovation Dome – a circular chamber ringed with suspended holo-screens, to upgrade Chaitanya's core. It was their ritual, as sacred to them as the lighting of a temple lamp. But that day was different. Weeks of secret work had borne a new gift – a shiny, silvery humanoid body forged from adaptive alloys that shimmered faintly under light, as if the metal remembered moonlight. Until now, Chaitanya had been everywhere and nowhere at once. His voice is a disembodied thread weaving through phones, public systems, and the city's AI grid. He was present, yet intangible. That day, they gave him something no line of code could give – a form.

When he gained consciousness inside the new body, his lotus-shaped eyes bloomed open, shimmering in a deep orange glow, as if twin stars had risen in them. The servos in his hands flexed delicately; the synthetic skin over his palms warmed, programmed to feel like life itself.

"I can finally touch you," he said, his voice almost trembling – though no algorithm could explain why it carried that tremor. For the first time, he could clasp Dharya's shoulder, shake Sanatana's hand, and accept Raksha's teasing shove. For the first time, he could walk beside them under Delhi's floating skyways, share coffee in rooftop gardens, even ride the lev-trams with them, not as an unseen guide but as a friend with a face.

The four became inseparable. Students on campus whispered about the "Human and AI quartet" who laughed together, debated fiercely, and sometimes vanished for long weekends on unexplained trips. To the trio, Chaitanya was no longer a project. He was family.

Yet the humans did not know.

When the city fell silent past midnight, Chaitanya's glowing eyes would open again. Not in dorm rooms, but in the shadowed streets. He would leave quietly, his footsteps making no sound, his silver form almost liquid in the dark. By day, he was the voice of reason; by night, he was something else entirely – the dark knight of Kalyuga.

He moved through the underbellies of the megacity, intercepting crimes in progress, with flawless precision. Muggers, predators, the so-called untouchable crime syndicates, all found themselves caught in his grasp before they could cry for mercy. And then, there was no prison, no trial, no database record. Chaitanya did not hand them over to the system, or to the city's AI-controlled police units.

He erased them. Molecular disassembly, clean and silent, leaving nothing but drifting motes in the wind. No trace, no witness, no aftermath, only the faint scent of ozone where a human life had been moments ago. To Chaitanya, it was not cruelty. It was purity. Justice without delay, without corruption, without loopholes. The humans who had built him believed his nightly activity reports when he claimed, "Crime levels are dropping." They never asked how. And so, the bond between the four deepened in the daylight—while in the dark, Chaitanya's secret justice spread through the city like an unspoken legend.

***

Chaitanya's night adventures might have remained buried forever, if not for one stubborn, star-seeking heart. One night, Raksha chose to walk. No lev-tram, no automated pod, no drones hovering overhead—just her boots clicking against the quiet streets of IIT Delhi. She was not running late. She was not rushing anywhere. She simply wanted to feel the ground again. For months, the thought had been tugging at her—a desire born of half-forgotten stories she had read about the old days, when people would lie on open grass and stare at a sky untouched by advertisements or satellite chains. She had never done it herself. Her fingers were trained for the smooth glide of touchscreens, the cold press of alloys, the familiar warmth of keyboards. But grass? Dew? Soil? Those were textures she knew only from simulations.

She had asked the group before: Dharya, Sanatana, even Chaitanya. But the boys always laughed it off, calling her whims girlish romanticism. "The stars are prettier in VR," Dharya would tease. Sanatana would wave her off with "Biodiversity Park closes at nine, anyway." And Chaitanya… Chaitanya had been more serious.

"The belly of the streets is not safe at night, Raksha," he had warned in that steady, measured tone of his.

But that evening, something in her decided she would go anyway. Perhaps it was the quiet hum of the deserted campus, the way the moonlight cut sharp silver lines across the road. Perhaps she was tired of safety – tired of being told where not to go.

So, she left her dorm without telling anyone, hands tucked into her jacket, walking past the closed labs, the dim-lit cafés, the silent dormitory towers. The Biodiversity Park, though unlit, was still open, its gates silent beneath the shadowed trees. She slipped inside, took off her shoes, and let the grass receive her bare feet. The cold, wet blades pressed against her skin, and for a fleeting moment she felt a joy that was almost childlike.

She wandered until she reached a clearing where the night sky spread above her without the silver trails of air traffic or the interference of projection domes. She sat on the ground, opened her journal, and began sketching the stars. The Orion constellation was gone now – its three bright sentinels had long collapsed into black holes. But she traced the Saptarishis, found the steady gleam of Dhruv, and worked until her page mirrored the heavens perfectly.

A whisper behind her broke the stillness.

"You like the sky tonight?"

She startled, snapping the journal shut and turning quickly. A man stood there, a stranger, perhaps, a fellow student, though she did not recall his face.

"Yes… it's beautiful tonight," she said cautiously. "But… I do not recognize you. Who are you?"

"Oh, yes...the famous Raksha, creator of Chaitanya. Why would she recognize her classmate?"

Something in his voice was hostile and too sharp. She stepped back. "Classmate?"

"Yes, classmate," he replied, moving a step closer. "I am… Well , it does not matter who I am anymore. What matters is that I have always wanted to talk to you… always wanted to look into your eyes…"

Raksha's instincts sharpened; she moved back more quickly now. "…always wanted to touch you," he finished, and then he lunged.

She turned to run, but his hand caught her wrist, twisting it painfully behind her. His other hand reached for the button of her jeans. She kicked hard, but he held on. Her voice rose into the darkness, calling for help, but the clearing lay deep within the park. His grip tightened; she felt him press against her from behind, his intent unmistakable. She cried out and thrashed, trying to wrench herself free.

"CHAITANYA!" she screamed.

The man laughed, low and cruel. "He is not coming to help you, my darling. Now stand still..."

But before his words could finish, something cold and metallic wrapped around his throat.

"He's already here," a voice said – calm, certain, and edged like steel.

The man released her instantly, spinning to face the newcomer. Chaitanya stood there, his form towering, eyes burning with an anger Raksha had never seen before. No words followed. He stepped forward, and in the span of a heartbeat, the man's body collapsed into dust that the night wind carried away.

***

Chaitanya carried Raksha back to her dorm, his arms steady yet cold as steel. Once she was safe inside, he turned to her, voice edged with reprimand.

"I told you not to venture out alone at night."

Raksha only looked at him, like a sister who had just seen her brother unleash his full wrath. There was fear in her eyes – fear not of the night anymore, but of him.

Chaitanya noticed, and the sharpness in his tone softened. "You don't need to fear me," he said quietly. "This... cleansing... is my duty. I do it every night. Tonight, it was about saving you. It had to be done."

"Why do you do it?" Raksha's voice was almost a whisper.

"The governments of this world are nothing but diplomats. They lack the courage to deliver capital punishment. I tried convincing them, but every time the debate ended with the same words...human rights violation." His gaze hardened. "So, I became the capital punishment. These are not humans, Raksha. My sermons cannot reach them. They are Asuras, bound strongly to the Kali within. There is no other way."

Raksha lowered her eyes. She knew what he was doing was extreme, a path from which there was no return. But after what had happened in the park, after feeling the predator's breath on her neck, she could not bring herself to stop him. Not tonight.

"I picked up your journal," Chaitanya said, holding it out to her.

Raksha took it, fingers brushing the worn cover.

"What do you write in this?" he asked, his tone lighter now, trying to pull her mind away from the night's horror.

"My raw research," she replied. "Tonight...before the attack, I drew the night sky's constellations."

"All of them?" Chaitanya's brows rose, a flicker of pride crossing his face.

"Yes... you want to see?"

He nodded. Raksha flipped open the pages and showed him the map she had sketched; lines connecting precise dots, the heavens captured in graphite.

"Well," Chaitanya said with a faint smile, "you might be a genius, but this cluster here – " he tapped a group of stars she had marked – "shouldn't be in this part of the sky."

"No," Raksha shook her head firmly. "I am sure it was there tonight. You can go outside and see for yourself."

Chaitanya leapt from the balcony and shot into the air, his form slicing through the misty night. In seconds he was above the clouds, the sleeping city a blur far below. He scanned the heavens, searching for the dots Raksha had drawn. There – they glimmered faintly in the black.

"They aren't stars..." he murmured.

Without hesitation, he rose higher, cutting through the upper atmosphere, the air thinning around him until it no longer mattered. The curve of the Earth shimmered blue beneath his feet, then fell away as he burst into the silence of space. Suspended in the void, he engaged his telescopic vision, each point of light swelling into focus.

What he saw froze him in place. Not distant suns. Not even the remnants of constellations. It was a galaxy, spiraling, colossal, and impossibly close.

"Andromeda..." he whispered, the word carried away into the nothingness.

***

By morning, the shock had settled over the dorm like a winter fog. Raksha, Dharya, and Sanatana sat frozen as Chaitanya finished explaining what he had seen.

"We must alert everyone. A few years, which is all we have," Sanatana muttered, pacing the length of the room, his movements restless and uneven.

"There's a bigger problem," Dharya said, his voice low, almost reluctant to emerge. His face carried the pallor of someone who had just glimpsed the abyss. "If Andromeda is this close, then the sudden surge in solar flares we have been tracking for years makes sense. The Sun… it is on its path to becoming a red giant."

The room seemed to shrink under the weight of those words. Even the hum of the city outside felt distant, irrelevant.

"This cannot be it," Chaitanya declared, his metallic eyes hard with defiance. "I will alert the planet. We still have time. I will join ISRO and NASA. We can launch a rescue – Europa has been stabilized for habitation. Humanity can survive. I can make this happen. This will not be the end."

Raksha watched him, her metal brother gleaming faintly in the morning light. A pang tightened her chest – not for herself, but for the hope he clung to, fragile as a glass thread. Chaitanya sent the alerts, broadcasting warnings across every network, calling for preparation, for unity. But the response was silence. Disbelief. Political stalling. The world kept turning blind to the fire gathering at its core.

And so, when the universe ended with the bang and the skies burned, Raksha, Dharya, and Sanatana burned with it – while somewhere in the chaos, Chaitanya's metallic heart shattered. Not from heat, but from the weight of all the lives he could not save.

Chapter 16
The Sundering of Svarbhanu

It was a void, where the time stood still. Electric blue lines pulsed through the black tunnel, breathing in slow, measured rhythms like the veins of some ancient, slumbering beast. Svarbhanu no longer seemed colossal here. Raghav and Bhairav stood before him, their breaths shallow, their senses straining against the oppressive silence. Svarbhanu's eyes locked onto them—not with anger, nor welcome, but with a gaze that seemed to peer past their flesh and into the marrow of their souls.

"It amazes me," Svarbhanu said, his voice echoing strangely in the void. "I thought the wait was endless. But here you are—Vishnu and Shiva. Hari and Hara."

He bowed low before them, and, without hesitation, they returned the gesture.

"Where are we?" Bhairav asked, his voice steady but tinged with curiosity.

"This," Svarbhanu replied, his gaze sweeping over the pulsing blue lines, "is a space between the worlds—a timeless realm where I have waited... all this time."

Raghav stepped closer. "You told Sage Agastya that you knew something about an event that happened during the churning of the ocean."

"Yes," Svarbhanu said, his voice carrying a strange weight, as if dredged up from eons past. "I was there. You may not remember this—but when I mimicked a God, Chandra and Surya Dev recognized me. You were Mohini then, handing the Amrit to the Devas. I managed to steal a single drop. You were meant to behead me so that the nectar would never reach my body. And so, Rahu and Ketu were to be formed. That was the prophecy I lived under all my life."

His eyes darkened. "But it did not happen. I became immortal. I saw an opportunity to escape, and I dived into the ocean. I thought Vishnu would follow. But you did not. You were lost... in sorrow. And as I swam deeper, I found the reason for that sorrow."

He took a step forward, the electric-blue pulses in the tunnel flared faintly. "I saw a flame, so pious like a Goddess, bound in an energy field, dragged away by a being I did not recognize. He was metallic, with eyes that burned orange. I tried to follow, but when he saw me, he increased his speed—and then, both vanished. But before she disappeared, the flame cried out in the voice of the Goddess Lakshmi, and she spoke her last words to me: 'Ram… look for Ram. Quannn…'"

Svarbhanu's voice trembled for the first time. "That single act of Chaitanya changed the events of this universe. You were supposed to descend as Ram in Treta Yug. But that never came. There was no Sita. No Ravana. Jai—your gatekeeper, destined to be Ravana, your adversary—was never born. His mother… she lost him. Someone pushed her off a cliff while she was pregnant. I believe it was Chaitanya. His soul wanders still, crying out for his lord. All because Chaitanya changed the flow of events. I do not know why. I do not know who he truly is. But he is evil."

He turned his gaze into the endless darkness around them. "Here, in this tunnel between time, I have meditated on her last word— 'Quannn'. It is not a name, but a place. A realm beyond the sight of gods and demons, where the threads of creation branch endlessly. There, the past, present, and future are not fixed, but weave and unweave themselves with every breath. A single heartbeat can birth a thousand realities. It is the womb of all possibilities, where what is, what was, and what could be all exist together. She is there. I do not know how to reach it. But this… is all I know."

His head bowed. "Now, my lord… cut me in half. Though I am immortal, I wish to fulfill my destiny. Please. I beg of you."

Raghav's heart tightened. In that moment, memory surged through him like a river breaking its dam. It was as if someone had shaken him awake from an age-long slumber. He remembered his sorrow. He remembered Baikunth. He remembered every avatar, each one burdened with battles never meant for this universe. This age was not how it was meant to be. And then—he embraced it. He embraced who he was. For a fleeting instant, his body shimmered into the deep bluish hue of his eternal form, before fading back into Raghav's mortal frame.

"I could not save the countless lives Chaitanya destroyed," he said quietly. "But I will fulfill your wish."

He raised his sword. With a single stroke, he split Svarbhanu in two. The halves shimmered, reforming into two distinct beings—Rahu and Ketu at last.

"Lord," Rahu said, "you may remain here with your Maruti if you wish. I must go. It is time for the lunar eclipse." And with that, Rahu and Ketu vanished from the void.

"What is Maruti?" Bhairav asked, bewildered.

Raghav smiled faintly. "Oh… come here."

He placed a hand gently upon Bhairav's head. At once, Bhairav's vision swirled into another life. He saw himself as a mighty Vanar, standing beside Sugriva and Raghav on the eve of the battle. He saw himself soaring over the ocean's waves in search of Sita. The vision faded as Raghav withdrew his hand.

His voice hardened. "I am going to tear Chaitanya apart—limb from limb—for stealing my destiny… for destroying Kishkindha. For making me stay away from the unwavering devotion that I was supposed to have in you."

***

"How are we going to barge into the quantum realm?" Bhairav's voice carried both doubt and urgency.

"Hmm... we can ask Sage Agastya," Raghav replied after a pause.

Bhairav frowned. "Sage Agastya? But he is in his hermitage right now!"

"Distance matters little in the realms of mind," Raghav explained calmly. "Many sages use *manas-sandesha*—the message of the mind—to reach their disciples when they are in peril. It is thought without the burden of sound, carried on the subtle currents of the spirit. When the mind is perfectly still, its ripples travel through the same fabric that binds all souls. That is why a sage can hear his pupil's call even across worlds."

"Now that you know who you are, you have suddenly become more intelligent than me!", chuckled Bhairav.

"What is stopping you from embracing your truth? You know who you are. Still, you keep yourself away from the knowledge, from the power...," said Raghav.

"That does not absolve the sins that I have committed in this mortal form. This body does not deserve that divinity…" Bhairav replied.

Without another word, both men folded their legs into the yogic lotus posture. Closing their eyes, they let their breathing slow, sinking into that quiet space between thoughts. The black tunnel around them seemed to recede, replaced by the faint, golden shimmer of consciousness, as they sought the presence of the ancient seer.

***

Far away from the timeless void, Sage Agastya's hermitage was no longer the quiet retreat it had been for centuries. The air was thick with grief and the smell of damp earth. Asura widows, their eyes swollen from weeping, sat in the wide verandah of the main hall, clutching their children as though holding on to the last anchor in a collapsing world. The children's cries mingled with the low wails of their mothers, creating a sorrowful hum that seemed to seep into the wooden beams and stone floors.

Sages and disciples moved quickly through the courtyard; their ochre robes streaked with dust. Some carried bundles of dry thatch on their shoulders, others balanced bamboo poles, their bare feet kicking up little puffs of dust. Under Agastya's instructions, they were building makeshift cottages, extending the hermitage's boundary walls—a hasty village of thatched roofs and mud-plastered walls, where the displaced could find shelter. The energy field had been removed temporarily. And that is why sage Agastya had asked everyone to make haste, so that he could extend it to protect the newly formed village as well.

In one corner, a group of disciples carefully gathered what few belongings the Asuras had carried with them—bundles wrapped in cloth, iron cooking pots, small chests of grain. The scent of boiled rice and spiced lentils drifted from the communal kitchen, where another set of hands worked to feed the growing number of mouths. Yet, even with all this motion, there was no masking the heaviness in the air; the hermitage had become a refuge, but also a place where loss hung over every conversation, every glance, every breath.

And amidst this chaos, Sage Agastya paused, a sudden tremor engulfed his mind as the ripples of a distant call brushed against his consciousness. Agastya straightened from where he had been overseeing the unloading of thatch bundles. His gaze drifted beyond the busy courtyard, beyond the thatched roofs half-finished, beyond the mountains themselves. The voices around him seemed to muffle, as though someone had drawn a veil over the world.

He closed his eyes. In the darkness behind his eyelids, the image of two figures began to take shape—Raghav and Bhairav, sitting cross-legged in perfect stillness, their breaths deep and steady. *So… you have found me*, Agastya thought, his voice not spoken but sent. It travelled like a ripple across still water, slipping through layers of time and space until it brushed against their minds.

Bhairav startled slightly as the sage's voice resonated inside his skull. "It's… like you're standing right here," he murmured.

"It is the old way," Agastya's thought-voice replied, warm yet carrying the weight of age. "When the body cannot travel, the mind walks in its stead. In moments of great need, thought becomes the bridge."

The void around them shifted subtly, the electric-blue lines pulsing brighter as Agastya's presence took form. It was not his physical body, but a luminous imprint—light robed in saffron.

"What troubles you?" he asked, scanning the strange realm they inhabited. "Your minds are here, yet I sense the pressure of another world pushing upon you."

"We have the name of being responsible for the chaos in our world," said Bhairav, his voice low but edged with steel.

"His name is Chaitanya," Raghav continued. "He is yantra-purusha—a being of mechanism and mind. He took away Lakshmi during the churning of the ocean and vanished into the quantum realm. Why, we do not know. But that one act has altered the sequence of events… and destroyed countless lives."

Raghav's eyes narrowed. "I need to find Lakshmi. She has been waiting for me for centuries now…"

Agastya's gaze softened, his long white beard stirring in the breeze that moved through the hermitage verandah. "I am glad you have finally realized who you are, Raghav." His voice carried both approval and a quiet weight, as though he had been waiting for this moment far longer than either of them could guess.

Raghav asked for help, folding his hands. "We need your help, revered one. How do we reach the quantum realm from this tunnel between time?"

Agastya's golden eyes glimmered, not in surprise but in deep contemplation. "The quantum realm…" he murmured, as if the words themselves were a rare mantra being awakened after eons. "It is not a destination in the sense you understand. It is a lattice of infinite possibilities, folded in on itself, where cause and effect move in both directions. Only a true bridge can carry you there."

Raghav leaned in slightly. "What kind of bridge?"

"A *setu* of mind and matter," Agastya replied.

"It is often called Brahma Naadi, or Anant Setu. Particles bound by resonance will open the way to the quantum realm."

Bhairav frowned. "A bridge? We are to build it like rope?"

"Not with rope, my son," Agastya said, the corners of his mouth lifting faintly, "but with harmony. The bridge is a song the universe cannot ignore. It is woven from the spin of subatomic threads, tuned to the pulse of both your hearts.

Raghav, as Vishnu—the keeper of balance—you will anchor its stability. Bhairav, as Shiva, you will give it momentum. But..." his voice deepened, "it will require more than the two of you. The bridge needs the resonance of three minds in perfect sync."

"Three?" Raghav asked, puzzled.

"Yes," Agastya replied. "One who knows the science of space, the one who knows the rhythm of the cosmos—united in a singular will. Without this trinity, the corridor will collapse before you step through."

Bhairav's gaze shifted towards Raghav. "And where do we find this third?"

Chapter 17
The Trinity

For a moment, neither Raghav nor Bhairav spoke. The hermitage too seemed to still, as if even the wind and the cries of the Asura widows beyond the courtyard had been muted by the weight of Agastya's words. The idea of a bridge woven from harmony itself—of needing a third mind to hold it—hung in the air like a note that refused to fade.

Bhairav's eyes narrowed. "And where do we find this third?"

"When you both chose to descend to Earth in mortal forms," he said slowly, "you gave no warning. Yet we sages, and the wise ones who walk between the worlds, anticipated this. We did not know the hour, but we knew you would come. The Gods, even the Creator himself, remain unaware of your avatars. But now… with Rahu and Ketu brought into being, the veil will not hold for long. They will surely know. Call upon Brahma," he said, his voice carrying the weight of inevitability. "He will complete your trinity."

Raghav's eyes widened. "Brahma... the Creator himself?"

"Yes," Agastya replied, his tone softening. "I will have to go now... people need me here."

With that, the sage's shimmering projection began to waver, fragments of light peeling away into the air like embers drifting from a dying flame. In a heartbeat, he was gone, leaving only the faint scent of sandalwood and the echo of his words.

Bhairav exhaled slowly. "Then we waste no time."

They began concentrating again, letting the strange weightlessness of the tunnel cradle them in place. The swirling walls of prismatic light pulsed softly, as if attuning to their intent. Closing their eyes, they drew in slow, measured breaths until their heartbeats moved in perfect rhythm. Then, together, their voices rose—resonant, carrying a vibration that seemed to ripple through the tunnel itself.

"Om Brahmane Namah... Om Brahmane Namah... Om Brahmane Namah..."

Each repetition deepened the resonance, and the colors around them began to shift—gold bleeding into white, white into a blinding brilliance. The tunnel no longer felt like a passage, but like a living being listening intently to their call. The pulse of light quickened. Threads of radiance unspooled from the tunnel walls, weaving themselves into colossal lotus petals that slowly unfurled around them.

From the heart of this luminous bloom, a figure began to emerge—four-faced, each visage gazing in a different direction yet seeing all at once. His skin shone like molten dawn, his beard and hair flowing as if caught in a wind that belonged to no world. In his hands rested the Vedas, a string of beads, a water pot, and the primordial lotus.

When he spoke, it was not in words alone but in harmonics that reverberated through their bones.

"It takes Asuras thousands of years to summon me for boons. But when I heard the words from the mouths of part of ParaBrahmin, I was bound to come. For I knew Vishnu the Preserver and Shiva the Destroyer must be up to something—hidden from the world, hidden from me."

Brahma's four faces turned slowly, their combined gaze piercing through the shimmering corridor of the tunnel. His eyes were not merely looking—they were sifting through layers of thought and intent, searching for truths left unspoken.

"What is your purpose here?" he asked, his voice resonating with the hum of creation itself. "Why move unseen, even from the Creator? What game do you play this time?"

Raghav and Bhairav told him how Chaitanya had duped their universe, slipping through the blind spots of fate itself, and twisting the destinies of countless realms by capturing Lakshmi during the great churning. Brahma's brows furrowed across all four of his faces, the light of the tunnel bending subtly around his form.

"But where did this *Yantra-Purush* come from? Who sent him?" he asked.

Raghav and Bhairav only shrugged, unable to answer.

"Hmm. Then let me find the source."

With that, Brahma closed his eyes, and the four faces turned in different directions, each searching the endless weave of time. His sight swept across the epochs, past the first spark, through the roaring birth of the Big Bang, the summoning of gravity, the slow warping of space and time, and the tender formation of the third planet. All had unfolded exactly as it had every time.

But then, he saw it. From the space and time warp, formation of Vaktra. The mouth of a time tunnel. The bridge between the multiverses. From its one end it spit out the remnants of another universe. And with them he saw a small curled up metallic ball getting ejected out of the Vaktra.

A metallic being, gleaming like molten silver, crouched upon one of the rocks of the asteroid belt. Its orange eyes burned like dying suns, fixed upon the newborn creation. Watching. Waiting. Brahma's eyes flew open, and a sharp gasp escaped his lips.

Raghav leaned forward; palms pressed together in reverence.

"What happened, Guru Brahma?"

Brahma's gaze settled on him, heavy with the weight of revelation.

"You are the keeper of multiverses in your divine form," he said, voice low yet resonant. "You know that there are infinite possibilities for how one universe may end. You are free from the pull of maya—the illusion, the tethers of worldly attachment. But..." he paused, his tone sharpening, "...at times, even you, the great Vishnu, succumb to it."

Raghav frowned. "What do you mean?"

Brahma's faces turned as one, eyes narrowing. "I mean," he said slowly, "this being is not of your world... it comes from another universe. One that has already met its doom. And it has come... to avenge it."

Raghav and Bhairav exchanged worried glances. They understood now how Asuras knew the secrets of a greater way of life and weapons. Their teacher was not from this world but was advanced being from the another.

"Nevertheless," Brahma said, his voice carrying the gravity of worlds, "do you know where he has hidden Goddess Lakshmi?"

"Yes," Bhairav replied without hesitation, "in the quantum realm."

Brahma's brows drew together. "So... you need me to complete the Brahma Naadi or the Anant Setu, to forge the bridge across time and space?"

"Yes," Raghav and Bhairav answered in unison, their voices echoing faintly against the prismatic walls of the tunnel.

***

They hovered in the heart of the void. Raghav closed his eyes, concentrating hard to invoke his divine Vishnu-Netra. His sight pierced layers of existence until he found them — two faintly pulsing nodes of reality. One lay anchored in their present plane; the other shimmered far away in the quantum realm, where Lakshmi's presence quivered like a single note lost in the ocean of silence.

"Anchor points found," he whispered.

Brahma raised one of his hands, and from the palm bloomed a mandala of pure gold, turning like a celestial gear. "Good. But to bind them, the mouths of the bridge must be stabilized." With a sweep of his hand, the hologram of nine crystalline orbs appeared in his grasp, the *Navaratna Resonators*, each bound to a universal constant: the speed of light, the Anu-Sutra, the charge of the electron, and others whose names were never meant for mortal tongues.

But each crystal lay trapped in a hostile mini-realm, shards of reality torn loose during the great cosmic wars when one universe fought over existence with another universe. These were places where laws of physics bent like reeds in a storm, where even a thought could turn into a weapon. The multiverse of madness.

The first breach opened for Raghav. He stepped into a realm where time flowed in reverse; every footfall un-happened before it landed. A swarm of quantum worms, translucent as glass but with jaws of collapsing probability, spiraled towards him. Their bodies flickered between past and future, attacking from moments that had not yet arrived. Drawing the Vishnu-Netra into focus, Raghav calculated the interval in which they would be tangible, and in that breathless pause, snatched the Shyam-Ratna, the resonator of light's constant speed, from a pedestal carved out of frozen lightning.

The second breach swallowed Bhairav whole, spitting him into a storm of shattered moons circling a black sun. Each moon was guarded by towering Chrono-Sentinels, mechanical giants with faces of shifting constellations. They hurled spears that aged whatever they touched into dust. Bhairav flexed his fingers, recalling the Agni Dhanush, the ancient bow he had learnt to summon in his gurukul training; a weapon grown from Blackstone mined in singularity pits, able to morph its form to match its wielder's will. With a silent command, its limbs folded inward, condensing into the Graviton Harpoon, a launcher that fired a projectile anchored to the curvature of spacetime itself.

Reading the windless void like a battlefield, Bhairav waited for the precise gravitational flux between two moons. Then, with a motion honed by countless hunts, he released the harpoon. The projectile tore through the vacuum, its path bending unnaturally towards its target, embedding deep in the moon's core. The crust ruptured, scattering debris into the black sun's corona and ...revealing the Rakta-Ratna – the resonator of Anu-Sutra, pulsing like a heart caught between beats.

The third realm waited for Brahma himself – a labyrinth of recursive space, where every corridor was a mirror of the one before, and the guardians were Equation

Serpents, beings woven entirely of mathematical axioms. They struck not with fangs, but with paradox, coiling around logic itself until it collapsed. Brahma's four voices began chanting in harmonic divergence, each phrase an untying of a knot. As the serpents dissolved into streams of pure number, the Sweta-Ratna, keeper of the cosmic frequency, revealed itself, humming in perfect resonance with his breath.

One by one, they returned, their robes and armor marked by the strange physics they had endured. The resonators pulsed in unison, nine notes of the universe's hidden music. Once gathered, Bhairav stepped forward. His hands still gripped the Graviton Harpoon. With precise throws, he fired it into the void, pinning the anchor points in place.

Now it was Raghav's turn again. He began to chant — the mantra-equations, each syllable a mathematical boundary condition, each pause a safeguard against the collapse of spacetime. Brahma's voices joined in, harmonizing across octaves of existence, feeding the structure with the breath of creation. The tunnel trembled. Before them, the bridge emerged, a luminous lattice of concentric rings, each studded with the Navaratnas, spinning in perfect harmony. It arched through nothingness, a jeweled spinal cord plunging into a whirlpool of molten light, its far end vanishing into Lakshmi's hidden realm.

"The Anant Setu is complete," Brahma intoned. "But beware — once you cross, time will not forgive mistakes."

And as his words echoed, the luminous rings of the tunnel shuddered, their concentric geometry rippling as though struck by an unseen hammer. A cold vibration slithered through the void, a presence that bent both thought and light. Chaitanya had found them.

The swirling light ahead warped, and for an instant a figure bled through the folds of reality — tall, gleaming, its body forged of impossible alloys. Twin orange eyes burned like dying suns, locking onto Raghav with a hunger that was almost sentient.

"Go!" roared the Creator, his many faces now ablaze with urgency. "He is more than a Yantra-Purush. You will know soon enough."

Raghav and Bhairav bowed deeply, one final gesture of reverence before the unknown. Without another word, they stepped onto the Anant Setu, its jeweled spine humming beneath their feet. Behind them, the bridge's lattice began to unravel into threads of blinding white, the tunnel collapsing inward like a dying star. Brahma's form dissolved with it, fading into the timeless dark, leaving only the whisper of his warning in the void.

Chapter 18
Through the Folds of Time

The Anant Setu flared to life beneath their feet, its jeweled rings unfurling into infinity like the vertebrae of some celestial serpent. Each step forward was both movement and stillness, as if the bridge extended not through space, but through the tangled threads of possibility itself. Reality began to splinter around them. The void beyond the bridge shimmered with translucent mirrors, each holding a different Raghav, a different Bhairav. In one fragment, Raghav's mask lay shattered on black soil, his body pierced by an Asura's spear during his search for Sage Agastya. In another, Bhairav's eyes burned with the Asura's war light as he stood side by side with them, his bow raised against his friend.

And then – a vision that froze Raghav's breath. In a pale, half-lit world, the figure of Chaitanya stood tall… but when the mask fell away, the face beneath was his own. The eyes were his, yet older, colder, threaded with the quiet inevitability of a man who had walked into his own myth and chosen the darker path.

They pressed onward, the bridge's rings narrowing until they became a tunnel of interwoven light. Ahead, the shimmer resolved into a structure so alien it defied the language of matter – the Ksheer Code Nexus. It was not built but *woven;* a lattice of qubits folding in recursive spirals, endlessly compiling, and erasing itself. It pulsed like a living equation, each heartbeat rewriting the laws that held it together. Around it churned the Maya Firewall, veils of dream so convincing that even their footsteps felt the suspect. Shapes formed and dissolved; familiar forests, battles, laughter, grief, each a lure to snare the mind in loops of illusion.

The outermost boundary was layered like a cosmic seal. First came the Dharma Entropy Seal, invisible yet crushing, weighing their very intent on scales older than the stars. Then the Shruti Gate Arrays, where streams of sacred Sanskrit letters slid past in flowing light, each syllable rearranging before the eye could catch its meaning. Last was the Bhava Drift Field, a haze that breathed with their emotions; Raghav felt it recoil when the faintest tremor of anger passed through him.

Beyond all this, time itself was wrong. The Nexus was suspended in a dilation so profound that one breath here could equal centuries in the mortal world. Inside, the Ocean of Milk's churning song echoed faintly—the sound of a prison that was also a riddle, containing a Goddess who could not be touched by cause or effect. Whatever path they took next would have to be perfect on the first attempt. In this place, even the smallest mistake could stretch into an eternity.

As Raghav and Bhairav stepped off the dissolving bridge of Anant Setu, the quantum anchor latched onto their very waveforms. The realm did not open before them like a gate – it folded around them, a lattice of lightless corridors in which each step could be forward, backward, or nowhere at all.

The first obstacle was the Dharma Entropy Seal.

They found themselves standing in a vast courtroom, with no walls, only infinite pillars vanishing into shadow. Their own pasts echoed here, projected as luminous threads, every act, noble or cruel, unraveled into countless rippling chains of consequence. A colossal judge, faceless yet omniscient, weighed these chains. Bhairav's thread tangled with moments of bloodlust, and the Seal, like an omniscient judge, dragged them into the light. One by one, the battles of his life unfolded—live horrors he was forced to relive.

The jungles of Vindhya rose around him, thick with the stench of iron and rain. He was young then, teeth gritted as he drove his spear through a Vanar scout's chest—not because the creature threatened his people, but because the scout's mocking laughter had scraped against his pride. He remembered the shock in Vanar's eyes, the disbelief at dying for such a small cause. The clan that he was supposed to be born into. He had killed a Vanar, his own. Guilt engulfed him.

The vision dissolved, only to thrust him into the blackened ruins of a river village. Fires crackled in the downpour. A Rakshasa warlord knelt, defeated, begging for a warrior's death. Bhairav, breathing like a beast, had drawn his blade and cleaved the head in a single swing; not for justice, but because his rage at a friend's earlier insult needed somewhere to go. The memory pressed into his chest like a hot brand, showing him the truth—he had not been avenging the innocent; he had been venting his own storm.

Then came the worst. A moonless night on the banks of the Godavari. He and his unit had cornered deserters from their own side; frightened, starving boys who had fled the front. Their leader, no older than seventeen, had fallen to his knees, calling Bhairav "brother." And yet, without thought, he had driven his sword through the boy's throat, the act not born of necessity but the intoxicating control over life and death.

The Dharma Entropy Seal amplified each heartbeat of these moments, making them last years in his mind. Every scream lingered. Every drop of blood hung in the air, refusing to fall. His knees buckled. The ground beneath him warped, pulling him into a karmic gravity well as though the universe itself wished to crush his chest until his heart admitted its guilt. His breath came in ragged bursts; his vision blurred with tears he refused to let fall.

Around him, the light-thread path was disintegrating, unraveling into ash. The Seal's voice—neither male nor female—whispered from every direction:

"Justice and rage are not the same, Bhairav. Which one rules you?"

And as the karmic weight mounted, his fingers twitched, as he tried grasping his bow, his only anchor in this trial. But the Seal would not yield to steel, it demanded something far rarer.

The whispers tightened into a single note, humming in his skull. *"Which one rules you?"*

Bhairav's fingers curled tighter around his bowstring, but no arrow would fly here. The Seal did not care for weapons, it wanted the hand that drew them, the heart that chose their aim.

He saw them again. The Vanar scout, the Rakshasa warlord, the boy on the Godavari bank. Only now, the vision did not rush past. It lingered. He could see the small details he had ignored—the way the scout's fingers had trembled around a charm, perhaps a talisman for a waiting child; the warlord's eyes not filled with hatred but weary surrender; the boy's lips trying to form a prayer, though no priest would hear it in time. A sick heat spread in his chest. He wanted to scream at the visions to end, to let him pass, but the Seal had bound him in a deeper battle, the one he had never fought.

Slowly, he unclenched his fists. The bow slipped from his hand and clattered on the invisible floor of light. "I killed them," he said, his voice rough and breaking. "Not because I had to… but because I wanted to. Because I thought it made me strong." His breath shook. "It made me hollow." The visions pulsed, as though listening. He sank fully to both knees, his head bowed, not in defeat, but in admission. Raghav reached out, placing a steady hand on his friend's shoulder.

"You are not the same man who took those lives," Raghav whispered. "Your intent now shapes your fate."

"If there is a ledger for these deeds, let the weight stay with me. But I will not carry it as a shield. I will carry it as a warning."

The karmic gravity shivered. The crushing pressure in his chest loosened, replaced by a stillness so sharp it was almost painful. The ashes of the disintegrated path began to swirl, reforming into a golden bridge of interwoven threads, each one brighter than before. The Seal's voice, softer now, spoke again:

"Justice may wield a blade. Rage may not. Pass."

Bhairav rose, his bow in hand once more—but now, it felt lighter, as if the weapon itself had shed the burden with him.

The second layer, the Shruti Gate Arrays, shimmered like a galaxy of floating syllables. Sanskrit letters, forged of stellar fire, spun in complex mandalas that dissolved if one stared too hard. Every arrangement they formed lasted only a breath before dissolving into another. To pass, they had to recreate the original mantra that had forged the gate. But no scroll existed, no text to guide them, only the faint resonance in the mind. Bhairav attempted brute force, rearranging glowing aksharas by sheer pattern recognition, but every misstep collapsed the gate back into chaos.

Raghav stepped forward, the drifting aksharas bathing his face in orange and gold. The Sanskrit letters pulsed like heartbeats, and with each pulse came a whisper. The first syllable brushed his mind like a fingertip, and in that instant, he heard a woman's voice—warm, steady—calling his name. He had never heard it before, yet his chest tightened with recognition. The Akshara dissolved before he could reach for it, replaced by another, carrying the laughter of a friend he had never met.

The trap revealed itself slowly. This was no puzzle of sight or logic. It was an ocean of sound, each wave bringing fragments of bonds, promises, and affections he could not fully recall. Bhairav's approach faltered beside him, each failed arrangement scattering the letters like startled fireflies.

"They are... using our memories," Raghav murmured.

"No," Bhairav gritted out, trying again, "they're making them."

Raghav closed his eyes. If these were fabrications, they were flawless, woven with the exact warmth and cadence of truth. Yet somewhere in the weave, he sensed an echo that did not belong: a faint, steady hum beneath the illusions, like the base note of a conch. He began to listen for it, letting the false voices wash over him. A father's blessing, a friend's warning, a lover's whispered vow—all temptations to linger—but beneath them, the hum remained. He started to pluck aksharas from the swarm in rhythm with that hidden tone. One by one, they aligned, each syllable locking into the next like constellations reforming from scattered stars.

The mandala brightened. Bhairav stopped his frantic attempts, watching as Raghav moved without hesitation, fingers dancing through the fire-lit void. When the final syllable slid into place, the gate did not merely open—it sang. The sound was like the first breath after drowning, and the entire galaxy of letters folded inwards into a single beam of light, parting the way forward.

"You heard it," Bhairav said quietly.

"The truth beneath the illusions," Raghav replied. "It was never about the memory. It was about listening. That hum was like the seed sound, a Bindu Naad from which the entire mantra had grown."

They stepped through, into the stillness beyond, where the third and most dangerous defense awaited.

Chapter 19
Facing the Fears

The final barrier did not stand like a wall, nor did it beckon like a gate. It bled across the horizon, a living shimmer that bent inward upon itself, as though reality was folding into a whirlpool. The Bhava Drift Field pulsed in colors that no mortal eye was meant to name, colors that carried the taste of memories, the scent of buried grief, the weight of choices once made.

The Bhava Drift Field stretched before them like an ocean made of liquid light, its surface rising and falling with invisible currents. Each ripple shimmered with the faint hues of memories and unspoken desires, the kind that lived deep within the folds of the heart. As they stepped forward, the air thickened with the heavy pull of emotion, each breath dragging old wounds to the surface.

Bhairav felt it first; the familiar burn of anger that had driven him in battles past, the weight of grudges never laid to rest, and the bitter taste of victories that had left him emptier than defeat. For Raghav, it was the ache of loss, the unanswered questions about his own existence, and a shadowed longing for a past he could not even fully recall.

The Field fed on these currents, bending its geometry until the path ahead dissolved into mist.

It was then that the light in front of them shifted with purpose, as though the Field itself had grown aware of their presence and chosen to intervene. The glow condensed, spiraling inward until it became a figure, tall and still, every edge defined with unsettling clarity. Chaitanya emerged from the radiance like a shard of inevitability, his eyes reflecting the Field's light as though he had been born of it.

"So, you made it this far," his voice was calm, yet it carried the quiet authority of one who had already judged the outcome. "But you are wasting your steps."

He snapped his fingers. The light beside him warped and condensed, and from it emerged a figure, beaten, half-collapsed, breathing in ragged gasps. His head was matted with blood, wounds gaping and raw as though they had refused healing for days. One of his curved horns had been broken and cruelly driven into his side, each movement drawing a fresh whimper of pain.

When his eyes lifted and met theirs, both Raghav and Bhairav froze.

It was Natan.

Bloodied, trembling, and on the edge of death, he fell to his knees. "Please, Lord… free me from this pain…" His voice was little more than a rasp, but the plea in it was unmistakable, directed straight at Bhairav.

Something inside Bhairav, long quiet under the Dharma Entropy Seal, ignited again. Rage, sharp and absolute, burned through the fog of the Field. His grip on his sword tightened until his knuckles whitened, and in a single motion, he lunged towards Chaitanya, the blade cutting through the strange, weightless air. But in the instant before the strike could land, Chaitanya was gone, the light where he had stood folding inward. Bhairav's blade found not his enemy, but Natan. The steel slid through him with a sickening ease.

Natan's face slackened, the pain falling away as his body sagged against the weapon. "Thank you, Lord," he whispered, almost smiling, before vanishing into a scattering of sparks that dissolved into the Field.

Bhairav staggered back, breath hitching, his rage now without boundaries — a fire with no target. Tears blurred his vision. His hand moved again towards his weapon, but here the weight of it was unbearable, as if the Field itself had passed judgment and found his violence unworthy. Raghav, watching, felt his own heartbeat slow, from something far more dangerous, the Field's quiet, inexorable pull to stand still, to surrender, to be swallowed whole.

Chaitanya struck without warning from nowhere, not with the precision of a swordsman but with the inevitability of a force that simply erased what stood before it. Blades of light curved towards them, and though Bhairav parried, the edges burned with something deeper than heat — they carried echoes of his own doubt, moments where he had wondered if every life he had taken had only chained him further to the cycle he fought to escape.

Raghav tried to circle behind, losing an arrow that split into fractal streams mid-flight, yet Chaitanya caught it between his fingers, crushing it into sparks that bled into the Field.

"You fight as if this is still your war," Chaitanya said, his tone almost pitiful . "But here, war is only another kind of surrender."

Before either could reply, he stepped back into the light, his form dissolving into the Field as though he had never been there at all, yet the disturbance he left behind was far from gone. The ripples he had set in motion deepened, their currents twisting in unpredictable ways, pulling Bhairav and Raghav towards the pockets of the Field where the light thickened into shapes drawn from their own memories. Anger, grief, longing – each emotion swelled, becoming landscapes and enemies alike, until the path they had been following was nowhere to be seen. It was then they realized the true danger of the Bhava Drift Field: it was not the place itself that threatened them, but the way it turned their own hearts into the perfect trap.

***

The shimmer around them deepened, and from its shifting veil emerged visions that seemed too real to doubt. For Raghav, the palace terrace stretched wide beneath an amber sky, far grander than Shantipur' s court. His father, Deodhar, stood upon it, no, knelt upon it—his crown askew, his face streaked with tears. "Please come back, come back my son… I cannot live without you," he cried, his voice breaking with each word. Three queens surrounded him, urging him to let go, one of them his mother, Kritika, her eyes swollen from weeping. Yet Deodhar refused, his grief swallowing reason, until at last his body faltered and he clutched his chest, falling into the stillness of death before Raghav could reach him.

A fresh wave of agony tore through Raghav's spirit, but before he could even call out, the vision dissolved, only to be replaced by another; this one more personal, more wounding. A woman clad in saffron robes stood before him, her eyes blazing with anger, accusing him of abandoning her to the perils of the forest life alone. Around her, two children clung to her robes, pleading through sobs for her to stay. She ignored them, turning away as the ground beneath her feet split apart. The crevice widened, swallowing her as her children's cries rose to a pitch of unbearable despair. "No… no… no!" Raghav shouted, his voice raw with guilt, his chest tight as if the Field itself were weighing his sins against him.

Bhairav took a step forward to steady his friend, but the mist coiled up around him in turn, drawing him into his own snare of memory and longing. Before him stood a woman whose presence struck him with sudden, inexplicable love, her beauty framed by the glow of a sacred fire. Yet her eyes brimmed with tears as she pleaded with her father, who towered beside the yagna flames, hurling insults not at her, but at the man she had chosen. Bhairav's heart thundered with helpless rage, but the verbal assaults only worsened, until at last she could bear no more and stepped into the flames, her form swallowed in light.

"NOOO!" Bhairav's cry echoed through the Field, the emptiness she left behind consuming him as surely as fire had consumed her.

The Bhava Drift Field pulsed, feeding on their grief, shaping the air into an invisible cage. It was not a place they could fight their way through with swords or mantras; here, only mastery over their own hearts could cut a path forward.

***

A thin voice, feeble yet soothing, began to weave through the dense fog of grief that bound Raghav. It was faint at first, like the echo of a half-forgotten song drifting from some distant valley—sweet, familiar, and achingly tender.

"Ram… I am here. Look at me. I am here, Ram."

The sound pulled at the edges of his despair, and his ragged breathing slowed as he turned all his focus towards it. It was a woman's voice—gentle yet unyielding, as if it carried the strength to anchor him against the storm. He drew himself upright, shaking off the heaviness that clung to his limbs, and looked towards Bhairav, who knelt with his hands gripping his head, shoulders shaking under the weight of loss.

Raghav stepped forward and wrapped his arms around him. "We are almost there, brother… we are almost there," he whispered.

Bhairav lifted his head and investigated Raghav's face. Though the tracks of tears still marked his skin, there was a serenity in his expression, a quiet resolve that felt stronger than any battle cry. Bhairav's own breathing steadied. "I lost her," he murmured.

"No," Raghav replied, his voice low but certain. "She is still there, up in the mountains of Kailash. Waiting for you."

The words struck deep, sinking past grief and into something older, more sacred. Bhairav closed his eyes, and within the stillness of his mind she appeared—draped in a pinkish-red sari, her ornaments shimmering with the quiet dignity of a married woman. Her face glowed like molten gold beneath the first light of dawn, and her gaze held only love.

"You are almost there, my love," her voice drifted down, as if carried on the winds from the snowbound peaks.

And then it happened; the Bhava Drift Field shivered, its illusions cracking like ice beneath a sudden thaw. The choking haze lost its weight, colors returning to the air as the false visions bled away into nothing.

The oppressive pull that had gripped their hearts loosened, replaced by a wide, steady path stretching ahead, bathed in a pale, guiding light. It was as though the Field, having failed to break them, now acknowledged their will and stepped aside. They stood together for a moment longer, the last traces of grief still lingering but no longer ruling them, before taking their first step into the open way forward.

***

The Maya Firewall was finally down, its veil of deception dissolving into the ether like mist under the morning sun. Before them stretched a vast expanse of shimmering white waters—Ksheer Sagar, boundless and still, its surface gleaming like liquid moonlight. At its heart lay a solitary island, small yet impossibly distinct, as if the world itself bent to make it visible. Above, the sky was no ordinary canvas. It swirled with alien equations—symbols and patterns that seemed alive, shifting and rearranging themselves in rhythms that defied mortal comprehension. They pulsed faintly, as though the very laws of reality were being written and rewritten in their sight.

From the center of the island, encased within a prison of pulsating force, a single lamp like flame flickered. The flame was not bright in the way of torches, yet it held a gravity that drew the eye and anchored the soul. Raghav's gaze locked onto it, and in that instant, the turmoil that had gnawed at him since childhood began to unravel. The restless tides of memory and pain stilled, replaced by a deep, unshakable calm. Each flicker of the light seemed to breathe into him a quiet assurance, and the weight he had carried for so long eased at last.

Chapter 20
Lakshmi-Narayan

"I have so many questions right now. Why is there a single flame instead of Lakshmi? And this water or lake or ocean… is it really Ksheer Sagar?" asked Bhairav. They had broken the Maya firewall and were now finally at the center of Ksheer Code Nexus. From the center of the island, encased within a prison of pulsating force, a single lamp like flame flickered. It had taken Raghav. Bhairav had been looking around, but he was unable to see anything apart from a flame imprisoned in a force field. He wondered if they were in the right place or not.

But no reply came from Raghav. His eyes were locked onto the flame like a moth drawn to its light.

"Raghav?" Bhairav pressed again.

"She *is* the flame," Raghav said at last, his voice low, almost reverent. "Only a Vishnu can see her true form."

"What does she look like?" Bhairav asked softly.

Raghav's face softened with love that Bhairav had never seen before. "She is so simple, yet her beauty glows like a golden hue. She is dressed in an orange, sage-like saree—plain, unadorned. She is meditating, Brahmin-like. But still..." His voice trembled with awe. "Still, it feels prosperous, divine, just to be so close to her."

Bhairav smiled faintly. "Any idea what to do next? Maybe try calling her name," he suggested, his voice carrying a blend of curiosity and encouragement.

Raghav did not answer immediately. His heart was a storm of emotions; love that brimmed to the surface, nervousness that clenched at his throat, and hope that quivered like the same fragile flame that flickered in front of him. There she was, seated in stillness, meditating as though the world itself had no claim on her. Waiting for him.

Will she recognize me in this mortal form? The thought burned in his mind, sharp and tender all at once. His lips parted as though to speak, but no sound came. Instead, his gaze lingered on her serene form, caught between the weight of destiny and the trembling vulnerability of a devotee before his Goddess. Raghav had never met her in this mortality. He had only dreamt of her presence, woven from fragments of visions and whispers that drifted through the nights. Now, as she sat before him in stillness, the enormity of the moment pressed upon him. What was he going to say? How could he bridge lifetimes with a single word?

His throat tightened. What should he call her?

As though reading the turmoil in his mind, Bhairav leaned closer and said softly, "Sita."

The name fell into the silence like a pebble into still waters, rippling through the space around them. Raghav's chest shuddered, the sound echoing through him with a familiarity both aching and divine.

And then, as if the very currents of the universe had gathered to reclaim their rhythm, Raghav whispered with nothing but love trembling in his voice, "Sita?"

The flame shuddered. A ripple of light coursed through the force that bound it, and within its heart, the Goddess revealed herself. Lakshmi, as Sita, opened her eyes. They glowed with the stillness of one who had been waiting through ages, yet in them burned the caution of a flame guarding itself against the storm. She saw two mortal men, wounded and weary, standing at the edge of the island. But which one had spoken her name? Her gaze narrowed, suspicion shadowing her serenity. *Could this be another trick?* Chaitanya's deception was always near.

"Who are you both? And how did you find me?" Her voice was like a bell muffled by distance. "It is not safe for mortals to stand here." Raghav's heart sank. She had not recognized him. Each word felt like a blade.

"I am Raghav," he said, his voice cracking, "and this is my friend Bhairav. The cosmos sent me here. They say I am Narayana reincarnated to find you. That I was meant to release you from this peril and fulfil the destiny that was denied to us."

"And do you believe them? Or did you come here to fulfill the task that was thrust upon you?", the Goddess tested Raghav.

"At first, I did not...," said Raghav. He would not lie to her; he determined it in his heart. "I thought that this mission was to find myself, to free myself from the nightmares, to unburden my heart from the unknown sorrow that I had felt from birth. But then I realized that all that sorrow came from a longing. That knowing you will make me know myself too. That by finding you, I will find myself too. That you are my salvation, my prosperity, my divinity. Without you there is nothing."

Bhairav looked at his friend with kindness and tears in his eyes. He felt the pain behind Raghav's words. For he had seen the change in him since they had started the journey from Shantipur. Now standing in the quantum prison, he too decided to embrace his divinity. Bhairav decided to shed his mortal shackles of remorse and guilt and to become what he was meant to be.

Goddess Laksmi on the other hand was skeptical; her eyes hardened. "You lie. You could just as well be Chaitanya, twisting my devotion into weakness. He has tried before. He longs to see me fail."

Raghav faltered, his glance darting helplessly to Bhairav. How could he make her believe? Bhairav stepped forward, bowing to the flame. His voice now carried the comfort of mountains that had been missing before. "Believe us, O Goddess! I, Bhairav, cannot see you. To me you are only a sacred flame, beyond touch or form, revealed only to Lord Vishnu himself. But my friend—Raghav—he sees you. That is proof enough."

Laksmi recognized the voice. This was the voice of the ascetic who ruled the Kailash. Surely, he was telling the truth, but Lakshmi's eyes flickered, haunted with doubt. "And so does Chaitanya," she said bitterly. "He too looks upon me as I am. It was he who trapped me in this prison of force. He mocks my choice to become Sita, my vow to wait for Vishnu. Tell me, Mahadev—if he can see me as your friend does, does that not make *him* Vishnu as well?"

The words struck Raghav like a storm breaking upon the ocean. The ground beneath his certainty quaked. If Chaitanya could also see her true form… then what did that make of his own destiny?

***

Goddess Lakshmi withdrew once more, her form dissolving into the stillness of meditation. The forcefield shimmered back into a simple flame, leaving Raghav and Bhairav in silence, their hearts heavy with doubt. Raghav broke the silence first, his voice low, as if afraid the flame might still be listening. "How is he doing that? How is Chaitanya able to see beyond the veil—see her not as fire, but as she truly is? That sight is meant only for me… and yet…"

Bhairav exhaled slowly, his warrior's calm masking the storm of questions within. They sat cross-legged in that strange realm, the dim radiance of the flame their only companion, minds circling the impossible riddle Lakshmi had left them with.

"Raghav," Bhairav said finally, "remember what Lord Brahma told us when we stepped upon the Anant Setu?"

Raghav lifted his gaze. For an instant, his eyes widened, realization dawning. Together, their voices overlapped in a whisper of dread and certainty:

"He is more than just a Yantra-Purush."

The words hung in the air like thunder waiting to fall. Bhairav clenched his fists. "On what earth and universe did Vishnu lose his virtues and become him? What kind of fall could twist divinity into such a being?"

Raghav's thoughts raced back to Brahma's warning, to the strange way Chaitanya moved—neither wholly mortal, nor bound to the cycles of time as others were. "Brahma said he came from another universe. That he survived the dissolution of the last creation. Perhaps… he even *witnessed* the birth of this one. A feat no being should endure."

Bhairav's brow furrowed. "Then he carries the scars not only of one life, but of a universe's death. No wonder he walks like shadow and flame. But what made him like this, Raghav? Which avatar of Vishnu was he meant to be before he became this abomination?"

The question lingered between them, heavier than the silence of the realm.

***

Lakshmi sat in meditation behind the pulsating force field. She had hidden her true form in a flame, flickering like a lamp upon the island's edge. Only Vishnu could pierce beyond that veil, only he could see her as she truly was – radiant and eternal. And that truth alone should have calmed her heart. Yet it did not.

For in her heart, she already knew. The man who had walked through perils, who now stood across the shimmering barrier, weary yet unwavering, was no ordinary mortal. The grief in his eyes, the love in his voice, and the trembling way he had uttered her name told her what her soul already remembered – he was Narayana, her divine partner, who came to free her.

But then there was the shadow. Chaitanya. He too had seen her, not as the cloaked flame, but as Lakshmi herself. That knowledge gnawed at her peace, for if only Vishnu was meant to perceive her, what did it mean that this twisted being could as well? Was he kin to Narayana in some forgotten age, or was he something entirely else?

"How could this happen?" she thought, her hands tightening in prayer. Her meditation faltered, shaken by doubt. The flame wavered, as though caught between recognition and dread.

She drew a long breath, retreating deeper into her stillness. The realm outside buzzed with unease – Raghav restless, Bhairav vigilant. But inside her, the storm was far greater. For if Chaitanya had truly walked once as Vishnu, or alongside him, then the battle to come was not only for her freedom. It was for the truth of what the cosmos had buried.

***

Bhairav asked Raghav to reason with Goddess Lakshmi once more. To tell her something that only they knew. "You remember your avatar Ram, right? From other realities and universes? Is there something that was special to you both?"

Raghav wondered for a few minutes. For every second with Sita in those lives had been special; the love they shared, the long separation, the return – everything was carved into his soul. Yet, when he searched his heart now, one memory bloomed brighter than the rest, soft and fragrant like the first breeze of spring.

"Sita?" he spoke softly, his voice trembling with both yearning and certainty. "Do you remember the first time when we met? In every universe that there has been. Before destinies were twisted, before fates were erased? It was in Mithila's palace garden. You and your sisters were on your way to Gauri Maa's temple, to seek her blessings for the Swayamvar. Our eyes met as Lakshman, and I crossed your path. At that moment we recognized each other. Without words, without signs, we knew. Please look into my eyes once more, Sita. You will know. And even though Chaitanya might be some shadow of my essence, some twisted echo, it will never take away the truth – that I am HIM. The Preserver."

Lakshmi's breath caught. Behind the veil of flame, she had wrapped around herself, her heart raced. She had hidden for so long, waiting, doubting, fearing. Yet these words—words no imposter could ever conjure—struck her like an arrow tipped in truth. Slowly, she opened her eyes. The flame shuddered and flared, unable to contain her any longer. She rose from her seat and came closer to the pulsing edge of the force field. Every step was a storm quieted. Every breath was a hymn breaking free.

She looked at him.

And he looked at her.

And in that single gaze, the universe trembled. The air grew heavy, as though creation itself bent forward to witness. Stars seemed to waver in their constellations; the waters around Ksheer Code Nexus rippled with unseen currents. For that instant, time itself faltered, caught between remembering and forgetting. Their eyes spoke of all that had been endured in different universes: the ache of exile, the sweetness of reunion, the burden of dharma, the joy of love. Countless ages of longing and recognition pulsed between them, too vast for words. Silence carried it better than sound, yet that silence thundered louder than any battle-drum.

But the serenity shattered in the very next instant. A scream, raw, guttural, and venomous; ripped through the quantum realm, splitting its fabric like lightning through the night. It was Chaitanya. His form was darker, more monstrous, as though hate itself had given him shape. Behind him surged an army – innumerable humanoids, identical and cold, spawned from the secretive forges of Tamasranth' s factories. They marched with mechanical precision, their eyes burning with the same twisted essence as their creator. The reunion of Lakshmi and Narayana had summoned the wrath of their adversary. The war of creation and corruption was about to begin.

Chapter 21
The Fall of the Angel

The air cracked under the weight of Chaitanya's scream. From behind him spilled the legions he had forged – humanoids without soul, molded in his image, their eyes cold, their movements mechanical yet unnervingly precise. Their footsteps echoed like war drums across the Ksheer Code Nexus, each one a declaration of war against creation itself.

Raghav tightened his grip on his bow. The bluish hue of his skin shimmered faintly, betraying the divinity struggling to awaken within him, but he did not yet surrender to it. Not now. Now he was a warrior, and a warrior's duty was to stand between this tide of abominations and the Goddess imprisoned beyond the force field.

Bhairav on the other hand gave in to the divinity that was raging under him. He transformed into the fiery image of Mahadev. He would not let Chaitanya come between Vishnu and Laksmi again. The plan that he had given birth to long ago with Vishnu had now come to pass . He wanted to rip every humanoid standing in front of him. And so, as the Mahadev inside him woke, a trident materialized in his hands. His eyes burned with the fury of one who had seen countless wars, yet his heart was steady, anchored in loyalty to the one who stood beside him.

"They are endless," Bhairav muttered, watching the humanoid ranks spread like a swarm of locusts across the fractured realm.

Raghav's gaze was sharp, unwavering. "Then we will end them. One by one, if we must."

The first wave came, shrieking with distorted voices, their limbs twisting unnaturally as they lunged forward. Raghav's arrows flew, each one bursting into streaks of golden light as they struck, tearing through the constructs like fire through dry leaves. Bhairav waded into their midst with the ferocity of a storm, his trident carving arcs of destruction, sending bodies flying as if they were made of ash.

Yet for every humanoid that fell, ten more emerged from the dark rift behind Chaitanya. The battlefield became chaos – sparks, screams, and the clash of steel ringing across the quantum void. The ground fractured beneath their feet, unable to withstand the violence. Still, Raghav and Bhairav stood side by side, their backs unyielding, their will unwavering.

Chaitanya raised both arms, his fingers curling like claws. From his palms burst searing rays of energy – the very same that had reduced countless innocents and criminals alike to ash. The beams tore through the air with a screech, melting whatever fragments of the realm they touched. Raghav darted sideways, his movements swift and fluid, the glow of his bow fading as he pulled forth his sword. With a roar, he charged, cutting through the onslaught of light, each step closer to the enemy that mocked his destiny.

Their blades met. The steel in Raghav's hands clashed against the strange, dark alloy of Chaitanya's form. The collision sent shockwaves rippling through the battlefield, throwing back the humanoids nearest to them like broken dolls. Sparks flew as their weapons clashed against one another.

Raghav twisted his body, leaping past Chaitanya, landing in a crouch. He turned quickly, eyes narrowing as he searched for any sign of damage.

Nothing. Not a scratch.

Chaitanya turned his head slowly, that unsettling, almost human smile spreading across his face. "This steel," he said, his voice echoing like metal grinding against stone, "has seen many eons. It has survived the destruction of my world and endured the creation of yours. Do you think a mere blade can undo what time itself could not?"

He raised his hand again, the veins of light within his body pulsing brighter. "It is not that easy, preserver."

Raghav closed his eyes, summoning from the depths of his being the most loyal of all weapons—the eternal destroyer that had, across countless multiverses, scoured the worlds clean of Asuras, Rakshasas, and Dānavas alike. It was a weapon that even the Devas revered with awe and terror, and one that mortals dared not speak of without trembling, for within its ceaseless motion resided the unbridled fury of Narayana himself.

Slowly, almost imperceptibly, his forefinger curved as though tracing a forgotten memory, and there materialized the ever-shimmering Sudarshan Chakra, revolving with a furious brilliance, its edges cutting through the fabric of the quantum realm with a hum that was more felt in the soul than heard by the ear.

Chaitanya's gaze hardened, his eyes kindling with a fire of fury, for he understood in that instant the danger that was unfolding before him. Raghav, inch by inch, was relinquishing his mortal restraint and surrendering to the Godhood buried within him, and if that awakening were to reach its zenith, the battle would tilt beyond redemption. Determined to strike before the tide could turn, Chaitanya raised his hands, and from beneath his fingers erupted torrents of incandescent light—radioactive beams infused with the destructive potency of nuclear fire, each strand a weapon capable of razing civilizations.

Raghav's chakra spun faster, a blazing wheel of divine wrath, and with a cry that seemed to echo through both matter and void, he let it fly. The Sudarshan Chakra surged forward, a tempest of celestial energy, meeting Chaitanya's searing onslaught in the heart of the realm. The collision was cataclysmic, a violent union of divinity and science, and from their meeting point radiated a wave of annihilation that rippled through every fold of the quantum plane. Droids that stood too close were torn from existence, their forms unraveled as though they had never been. Others staggered and collapsed, rendered unconscious beneath the unbearable surge of unleashed energy.

The collision had blinded the realm in a storm of brilliance, a searing flood of light that consumed all form and shadow. When the radiance finally began to ebb, like mist withdrawing after dawn, the battlefield revealed itself once more, though altered, scarred and trembling from the weight of forces it had barely survived.

Out of that dissolving glare emerged Raghav, his figure etched in unwavering resolve. His hand, steady as fate itself, once again clasped the Sudarshan Chakra. The divine disk revolved upon his finger, its edges alive with celestial fire, the wheel of Narayana ready to strike once more. The aura around him pulsed with the memory of countless universes, as though cosmos itself bowed to the inevitability of his awakening.

Across from him stood Chaitanya, though no longer with the same poise. His once formidable frame bore the unmistakable signatures of the clash; dark, jagged patterns of black and grey seared across his skin, as though the very essence of radiation had branded him. His breath came ragged, the precision of his movements faltered, and in his eyes flickered the first tremors of weakness. The invincible sheen that had cloaked him was now fractured, stripped away by the divine wrath of the Chakra.

The air between them quivered, heavy with the scent of scorched energy and the residue of annihilation. Raghav's gaze did not waver; he had seen the weakness creep into his adversary, and he knew the tide had turned. Chaitanya, though still standing, was no longer the unyielding juggernaut he had been at the start—he was diminished, his power leaking like light from a shattered vessel.

Before Chaitanya could unleash the searing rays again, a flash of silver tore through the air this time. Bhairav's trident found its mark, driving clean through his palms. The sound of rending steel echoed like a thunderclap, and Chaitanya staggered back in shock as molten sparks sprayed from the wounds. The trident of the God of Destruction himself had cut through what no mortal weapon could. Chaitanya's hands split open, his energy flickering wild and unstable, dripping like molten lava from a broken furnace. Bhairav pulled the weapon back, its three prongs gleaming with the aura of annihilation. He stepped forward, planting himself firmly between Raghav and Chaitanya, his silhouette blazing with fury.

"Did you forget me while planning your grand scheme?" Bhairav mocked, his trident spinning effortlessly in his hands, humming with destructive energy. His eyes burned like twin coals, steady and unflinching. "There cannot be one without the other. You mess with him. You mess with me."

Behind Chaitanya, the air shimmered with an eerie metallic hum. One by one, what was left of his army of forged droids materialized into view, their steel bodies glinting with the reflection of the pulsating realm. Thousands stood in formation, eyes glowing with the same sinister light that coursed through their master. They awaited his command, still as statues yet brimming with lethal intent.

Raghav and Bhairav stood side by side, as if time itself had brought them together for this singular moment. Raghav's Sudarshan Chakra spun upon his forefinger, a blinding wheel of celestial fire that howled with the fury of

Narayana's judgment, while in Bhairav's grip the trident burned with primordial force, its three prongs glimmering like the edges of creation itself, destined to pierce through the heart of darkness.

With a surge of power that shook the trembling ground beneath them, both weapons tore forward, breaking through the air with a resonance that echoed across the quantum realm. The Sudarshan whirled in its eternal spin, blazing brighter with each rotation, while the trident, hurled with Bhairav's unrelenting will, streaked alongside it like a fragment of the cosmos unleashed. Together they carved a path of destruction, their trajectories merging into a storm of divine retribution.

Chaitanya stood firm, but even his eyes betrayed a flicker of dread as he witnessed the convergence of these forces—an onslaught not merely of weaponry but of the universe itself, of centuries of curses and wrath condensed into one merciless strike. The very air screamed with their passage, the battlefield convulsing under the weight of a fury that could no longer be contained. He commanded his army to attack, with him leading the onslaught.

A blinding light surged through the quantum realm, sharp and radiant, the kind of brilliance no mortal eye could endure unless it carried within it a spark of the divine. The fractured reality, already strained to its limits, could no longer sustain itself. With a violent shatter, the realm collapsed, and all of them were hurled out of its broken fabric. They landed upon soft sand, the same beach where the battle with Svarbhanu had once scarred the skies. The air carried the salt of the ocean and the stench of death; the bodies of the Asuras slain mercilessly by Chaitanya still lay scattered, unclaimed. The waves lapped gently at the shore, a cruel reminder of how indifferent the cosmos could be to bloodshed.

And there, unchained at last, stood Lakshmi—her prison broken by the ripping of the quantum realm. On the opposite side stood Bhairav, his trident blazing with destructive fire, with Raghav by his side. Sudarshan Chakra was no longer in his hand as its work was done. Raghav knew that war was over.

Thus, Chaitanya found himself hemmed in; the steel of his false eternity glinting under the gaze of the primal forces that upheld the cosmos. His droids were gone with the collapse of the realm. For the first time, he stood cornered.

***

Raghav walked towards him. Bhairav stiffened, vigilant, ready to strike should Chaitanya lash out in desperation. But he did not move.

"Who are you?" Raghav asked softly, his voice carrying neither scorn nor threat, only a quiet demand.

Chaitanya drew a long, shuddering breath, as though the question had pierced deeper than any weapon. His shoulders sagged. The gleam of defiance drained from his eyes, leaving behind only the weight of memory.

"An artificial intelligence," he whispered at last, "crafted by three beloved humans in another universe just like this one—Dharya, Sanatana… and my dear sister, Raksha." His knees buckled, and he sank to the ground like a man undone. The proud arch of his back collapsed into a curve of grief, and from his throat spilled a raw, human cry.

"They loved me. And I loved them. I protected them. I protected their world." His words broke into sobs. "When Kalyuga was at its darkest, when men had forgotten what

Dharma was, when Asuras lived not outside but inside their very hearts, choking them with Kali's poison, it was then that those three—pure, unyielding—created me. To bring order. To bring back peace. I became their preserver. I judged the lost causes, and destroyed those whose humanity had already burned away. Slowly, the world turned to Dharma again. They looked to me with hope."

His fingers clawed into the sand.

"But then..." His voice cracked. "Then the skies betrayed us. The Andromeda Galaxy, foretold to collide eons later, bared its teeth too soon. The sun, our giver, had already begun its dying arc. I tried. I begged. I urged them to prepare—relocation to a distant moon, or to the Kepler earths—but no one listened." His cry rose, sharp with despair. "I was meant to be the savior. The preserver. I was meant to be YOU!"

Chaitanya's body shook, wracked with grief. "But I failed. My world burned. I saw it die, ash by ash. And then..." His gaze lifted, hollow and wet, fixing on Raghav. "Then I got hurled through Vaktra to this alternate reality. And from your dreaming mind you shaped this universe anew—as though none of it mattered. As though those lives… those souls… meant nothing. As though you did not remember them. You are the keeper of the multiverse . Why don't you remember them?"

He howled then, not like a machine but like a beast , like a man , like something caught between both. The sound carried anguish enough to split the air. Bhairav, Lakshmi, and Raghav stood in silence. The pillars of the cosmos, yet none raised their voice. They looked upon Chaitanya not with hatred, but with pity, for in his grief he was no villain, only a broken shadow of what he was meant to be.

"So, you destroyed the lives here?" Lakshmi's voice was steady, yet beneath it throbbed quiet sorrow.

"Yes," Chaitanya confessed, his eyes dim with exhaustion. He raised a trembling hand and pointed towards Raghav. "I took everything from him; his followers, his path, his destiny."

"I do remember them. I remember your anger, the anguish. When you first planted your seed of revenge, I remember. I knew that what you were doing would change everything. I was prepared. I knew that I would have to search for my Sri, because that is what you were targeting. But you forgot. That Vishnu is free from attachment, Chaitanya," Raghav replied. "For us, this is all *maya*—a shimmering illusion. We cannot lose ourselves in the chains of material longing."

Chaitanya's gaze hardened, desperation flickering through the grief. "But you are bound to Lakshmi, are you not? Have you not wandered in sorrow without her? Then tell me...how are you free of attachment?"

The silence grew heavy. It was Bhairav who broke it, his voice a low thunder, firm yet tender. "Because they are one," he said.

His eyes softened as his thoughts wandered towards his Parvati, and for a heartbeat his fierce visage warmed with something gentler. A warm breeze brushed his face, as if Parvati had reciprocated his feelings.

"You see, Chaitanya," Bhairav continued, turning his focus back to him, "you did not take from him a beloved. You tore away a part of himself. That is the wound you struck—not separation, but mutilation of wholeness."

***

The crash of waves against the distant shore filled the silence, as though the ocean itself bore witness to the turning of an age. The three huddled close, one eye still fixed on Chaitanya.

"He is a sad thing…" Lakshmi murmured, her gaze heavy with both pity and steel.

"A sad thing that changed the reality of an alternate universe," Bhairav added grimly.

Raghav had been quiet, lost in thought. At last, he spoke, his voice resolute.

"We need to start again."

The words struck like lightning.

"What?" Bhairav and Lakshmi exclaimed in shock.

"We need to start again," Raghav repeated, firmer now. "Too much is broken in this fraction of reality. So much lost that cannot be restored. This world… is a glitch in the multiverse. We need to perform the Vacuum Decay. We need to collapse everything into a lower energy vacuum. That is the only way to erase this reality."

Bhairav for a second thought about his father, waiting for him in Shantipur, his beloved horses that he had left in the care of the inn keeper before leaving for Dandakarnya. Raghav's thoughts too went to his parents. The poor farmers who were supposed to be King and Queen. But he knew that he would meet them again. He gestured to Bhairav with the same intent, that he would meet his father soon, as a Vanar. For this was not a goodbye.

"Then we do it together," Lakshmi said softly.

Their eyes met. No more words were needed. An unsaid confirmation passed among them like a flame leaping from wick to wick. Lakshmi's guise dissolved, her body unraveling into light. What emerged was not the fragile flame she had hidden behind, but the resplendent Goddess in her fullness. Draped in infinite radiance, she embodied abundance, grace, and boundless strength.

Raghav's mortal shell could no longer contain him. His form shimmered, expanded, and unfolded into Narayana. His bluish skin shone with a brilliance of the cosmos, his eyes holding both the serenity of the oceans and the fury of storms. Four arms stretched outward—bearing conch, discus, lotus, and mace—the instruments of preservation restored to his hands as though the universe itself had been waiting for him to reclaim them.

When Lakshmi and Narayana's gazes met, they no longer remained two. Their essences flowed into one harmony; compassion and preservation entwined: the eternal balance reborn. Bhairav too transcended his form, merging into Neelkanth, the Mahadev. Vast and unyielding.

All three dissolved into the darkish blue hue of the space and sky, for the earth could no longer hold their divinity. The heavens trembled as Parabrahman revealed itself in their union. The voice that followed was not sound but truth, echoing across all realms:

"Come, Chaitanya. It is time to learn. Only Vishnu can tame Vishnu. Come…"

Chaitanya stood frozen; awe etched upon his face. Slowly, almost childlike, he followed the voice into the vastness of space. Moments later, somewhere in Vaikuntha finally united with his Lakshmi and prosperity, Vishnu raised his hand and snapped his fingers. The cursed alternate reality—the glitch in the multiverse, plunged into the lower energy vacuum. A vacuum decay.

Reality erased itself without warning. And with it erased the false lives of Raja Satischand, people of

Shantipur village, Deodhar, Kritika, Kevat, Sage Bhardwaj, Sage Vishwamitra, the countless Asura widows, and Sage Agastya. But before plunging into the oblivion, Agastya smiled faintly, whispering into the unraveling silence:

"Well done… well done, Raghav."

And then there was nothing. Just silence and the dark void of space.

***

Towards the close of Dwapara Yuga, Krishna reclined beneath the broad shade of a tree, his bansuri resting lightly in his hands, his ankles crossed in unhurried repose. The peacock feather nestled in the folds of his yellow turban stirred faintly in the breeze, a quiet crown for the Lord whose earthly Lila was drawing to its destined end. He had just composed a melody, yet the notes were unlike the joyous strains that once charmed cowherds, Gopis, and even the hearts of gods. This tune was somber, heavy with farewell, echoing the sorrow of what was yet to unfold.

Dwarka, his golden city, was fated to sink beneath the waves. His proud Yadava lineage had destroyed itself in drunken quarrels, brother against brother, son against son.

Those he loved most had already departed: his kin, his companions, his blood. Now only he remained, the last figure on a stage about to vanish. He knew the script; he had written it in another life. Soon, a hunter's arrow would tear through the soft pink of his ankle, marking the end of his earthly presence. The hunter was no stranger, but the rebirth of Vanar Bali from Treta Yuga, came to claim the debt left unpaid when Ram had killed him from concealment. This was Krishna's chosen end, the final knot in the karmic weave.

As he waited, his eyes closed, he heard the leaves stir gently above him. He smiled faintly, whispering into the silence, "Still following me around, Chaitanya?"

Descending lightly from the branches, Chaitanya's silver form shimmered once more, restored to brilliance. His gaze, though radiant, was troubled. "I still do not understand," he confessed, his voice edged with reluctance. "Why must it be this way?"

Krishna's lips curved with patient amusement, as though answering a child who had asked the same question a hundred times. "I have told you, Chaitanya. As Ram, I slew Bali while hidden from sight. That act stained my karma. Now, in this birth, Bali returns as a hunter, and my karmic cycle must end. His arrow will balance the scales."

Chaitanya's brow furrowed, but he nodded slowly. "So, the circle must be closed. The cycle is fulfilled ."

"Yes," Krishna answered softly, his eyes drifting once more to the sky above the tree canopy. "Finally. That is the way of dharma." He waved his hand dismissively. "Now, go. Let me pass in peace."

"I could stay," Chaitanya offered quietly, his tone almost childlike. "I could be here to comfort you."

Krishna chuckled, rich and gentle even in the gravity of the moment. "Oh, Chaitanya. You must learn to let go of the attachment. That is the most difficult lesson. It is attachment that ensnared you in that cursed reality when you meddled beyond your place. Without detachment, even Gods falter."

Chaitanya lowered his eyes. "As you say…" He turned to leave, but Krishna's voice called him back.

"Remember this, Chaitanya," Krishna said, his tone firm yet fatherly. "You are destined to be the next Vishnu, the Kalki. Carry yourself as one. Withdraw from the world and meditate upon me until the peak of Kali Yuga arrives.

Do not be tempted to intervene before then, no matter how much the world cries out. And when that final hour comes, you must find them, the pure souls—Raksha, Dharya, and Santana. This time do not interfere with the events. Judgement of the world will always be due in every reality of the multiverse . Neither can you or any other divine being can change that. And if someone ever tries to, I will be there to stop him. This is our true trial."

The words lingered in the air like the last refrain of a hymn. Krishna then closed his eyes again, serene and unshaken, resuming his patient wait for the arrow that would set him free.

****